This Ol' Casa – Building in Baja 101

A Layman's Guide to Building a Baja Dream Home

C. Phil Osso

iUniverse, Inc.
New York   Bloomington

This Ol' Casa—Building in Baja 101
A Layman's Guide to Building a Baja Dream Home

iUniverse books may be ordered through booksellers or by contacting:

iUniverse
1663 Liberty Drive
Bloomington, IN 47403
www.iuniverse.com
1-800-Authors (1-800-288-4677)

Because of the dynamic nature of the Internet, any Web addresses or links contained in this book may have changed since publication and may no longer be valid.

ISBN: 978-1-4401-26758 (pbk)
ISBN: 978-1-4401-26741 (ebk)

Printed in the United States of America

iUniverse rev. date: 02/18/2009

This book is dedicated to my clients, and my family, without whom none of this would have been possible. Special thanks to John and Ellen for the continued support and friendship.

TABLE OF CONTENTS

INTRODUCTION

This book is intended as a primer for those interested in building a home in Baja, Mexico. It's written in an easy-to-read style, and eschews technical jargon and specialized verbiage. It's for laymen, ordinary folks who want a roadmap to follow from the point they go out looking for land, to the point they accept delivery of their finished home.

To my knowledge, no such resource exists for those wishing to build a house in Cabo or the outlying areas. There are plenty of real estate publications espousing the virtues of buying lots or homes, and a fair number of guides describing the purchase and *Fideicomiso* process, but nothing that tells you how to go from the idea, "It would be awesome to have a home here!" to a finished house that reflects your desires and imperatives. That's astounding to me, as there are so many folks coming to the region with the idea of creating their own special place in paradise.

The idea of a, "Building in Baja for Dummies" approach came to me as I was winding down writing my column for the *Gringo Gazette* in Cabo. That column was entitled, "This Old Casa", and featured a bi-weekly thousand words, offering advice and warnings about navigating the sometimes treacherous waters of Baja home building. It was well received, and the original twelve column concept was extended to run forty-five columns.

As I concluded my involvement, it occurred to me that no definitive guide existed for ordinary folks to use when going through the lot selection, designer selection, plan creation, and home building process here. That seemed a negative, as there are so many horror stories which could have been easily prevented with a little planning and diligence. So, with columns in hand, I decided to undertake the first edition you're reading. It's by no means exhaustive, however it isn't intended to be. The goal is to give you enough usable knowledge to keep you out of serious trouble, and to ensure you have adequate information to avoid being taken to the cleaners by unscrupulous operators. If you follow my advice, you should be able to get through the process with minimal headaches, and you'll have a far better grasp as to what's actually occurring than most who shell out their cash to build in Baja.

The target audience for this work is the person interested in a medium to high quality dream home. What this book isn't is a guide to building the cheapest structure possible, or a way to do it yourself, or a magical formula for getting things done for half the cost of your neighbors. If that's your interest, best to look elsewhere, as you'll be deeply disappointed. No, what this little tome is intended to do is offer a step-by-step description of what you can expect, what to watch out for, what to do, what to avoid, when building a home here using qualified contractors and designers.

It's organized in a linear fashion, starting with advice on choosing a decent lot, and then moving to selecting a designer, getting the design you want, selecting a builder and inking a meaningful contract, and then building the house. Along the way I'll impart tips, opinions, preferences, and cautions. You're free to take them to heart as they resonate with you, however I would think twice about discarding the cautions out of hand. Most have been forged through harsh experience, and I offer them up with sincerity. Building down here has killed more gringos than malaria has, and the goal is to keep you on a safe road so you don't become one of the statistics.

With that aviso out of the way, let's start with some basics you should get comfortable with before you do anything.

First, understand that there are many reputable, sincere, conscientious designers and builders working in Baja, who will do everything they can to create a special home for you. Unfortunately, there are also quite a few larcenous or inept operators whose life mission is to separate you from your money while delivering as little value as possible. It's very much like the rest of the world in that respect. Any time the money involved is great, the white sharks will come out and attempt to bite off your arm. Just accept that, and keep it in the back of your mind as you proceed. It's sort of like walking through a remote neighborhood at night – you don't have to be scared, but you should keep your wits about you and stay alert, as the predators like to feed in the dark. They'll generally pick on the weak or the unaware, preferring easy targets to tough ones.

If you're reading this, you'll be one of the tough ones by the time you're done with it. That's part of the goal – to make it extremely difficult to bamboozle you.

Second, understand that this is a different country with its own pace and cultural mores. It may seem like a colorful suburb of San Diego at times, but it isn't. Aside from the language, the two most different things about the place are the sense of urgency, and the reluctance to deliver any sort of bad news. Both are part of the package, and I can tell you with complete sincerity that it's impossible to win a battle to change those.

One of my Mexican friends has a saying, which you should take to heart: "The Mexicans Always Win." He means it in a resigned and friendly way, not in a negative way. A loose interpretation would be that the locals have a better sense of how things work here, and how long things actually can take, than you do – and any efforts to alter the process or fight it are doomed to failure. Especially in any sort of altercation or disagreement, they can wait you out. Disagreements can take years, or decades, to resolve here. That's dissonant to the Gringo ear, as we tend to be very deadline oriented, and are a generally impatient breed. Baja natives are patient. Very, very patient. They have to be. Until just recently, roads routinely shut down, power went out for long periods, consumer goods were sporadically available.....if you weren't patient, you'd blow a gasket and be carried out in a body bag.

The Mexican culture places a huge premium on politeness in interactions, to the point that bad news is generally avoided, as it would be upsetting to the recipient - and that would be impolite. That means that if there are problems or delays, you won't hear about them until the last possible instant. There's a reason for that, culturally-speaking. If one waits long enough the problem might just go away due to natural causes – one could be dead tomorrow, so why visit tomorrow's problems today when nature might offer an out, and the unpleasantness of the problem can be avoided? Baja teaches you that things can change quickly. Just consider the number of highway memorials for proof of that, or reflect upon the fact that the number one cause of death in Baja for Gringos is traffic accidents. I've personally almost expired about five times on the highway between TJ and Cabo, none of the incidents my doing, so I can assure you that the menace from the road is very real. But the point is that there's a greater sense of the temporary and transient nature of life here in Baja, thus tackling the unpleasant today is the last thing anyone wants to do. Procrastination is a time-honored pastime, and you aren't going to change that. So don't expect anyone to volunteer info on problems. It doesn't happen.

Another friend of mine, who's lived here for over two decades, has a saying that's absolutely and frustratingly accurate: "If it wasn't for the last minute, nothing would get done." That's also true, for the same reasons. Why do the hard thing today, if it can be put off 'till tomorrow? That attitude results in projects running perennially late, with problems put off 'till the last possible minute, leaving little time for anything but crisis management. It's not a great way to run a railroad, but it *is* the way this Baja train generally careens down the tracks, so best to understand the animal you're dealing with.

For the same politeness reason, most yes/no questions will be answered with five minute allegorical responses if the news isn't good. "Did you finish polishing the floor?" will be met with a description of the process, an explanation of the care required to do a good job, perhaps a story about an illness in the family or a tragic injury or a broken down car. It is never just, Yes or No. Again, that's the lay of the land, so learn to deal with it. The way I do it is simply to listen patiently, and then repeat back to the respondent what I think he meant – Yes, or No. If I am correct in my interpretation, I'll get a sheepish indicator in the affirmative.

Probably the most frustrating thing is the way *really* bad news is avoided. Oftentimes, cell phones will just cease ringing for days at a time when a contractor doesn't have whatever they were supposed to supply ready. They'll just go dark on you. Again, it's the way things work in Baja, so you need to understand that it isn't personal.

Building in Mexico is as much an exercise in immersion into the culture as it is constructing a residence. What you'll learn as you go through the process is how the Baja world works, for better or for worse. Many of the endearing attributes you love about the area can be double edged swords when you try to accomplish anything besides opening a beer – relaxed, *manana* lifestyle isn't necessarily consistent with highly efficient, on-top-of-things building. So you need to be aware of the current you're fighting as you navigate the waters, and bear it in mind as you make critical decisions regarding your project.

That's the quick overview of the cultural landscape. I put it right up front, as understanding the characteristics of the culture is key to getting a successful outcome. You need to be crystal clear on what you're dealing with as you go through these pages, as many things will seem obvious coming from the United States or Canada – but they aren't givens here. Assumptions as to how things "should" work are very dangerous, as many things don't function the same way as back home. The road rules are different, the language is different, the bureaucracy is different, the culture is different. That's why a recurring theme in my writing is that you need to do your homework so you understand what you're working with, and don't take anything for granted. Information is power, and the more you know, the better your decision-making, and the more critical your eye will be.

In summary, the first thing you need to remember is that you aren't back home in Kansas, and that things don't operate the same way here as they do there. The second thing to remember is that there's no safety net to catch you if you fall. Your best and only defense is to understand as much as possible about what you're doing, as there's little to no recourse for you if you make serious mistakes or allow yourself to be taken advantage of.

Which is what this book is all about. Training your senses so that you can spot the landmines before you step on them, and can't be flim-flammed or tricked in any of the myriad ways that are possible when building a house, "Down Mexico way." Stick with me, and you'll be armed and dangerous by the time you're done reading.

With that in mind, let's get to it.

CHAPTER 1 – THE LOT

Mexico. Land of *mariachis*, breathtaking sunsets, dazzling blue water, ice cold *cerveza* and *margaritas*, white sand, balmy weather, a relaxed, "No worries" attitude.

Things are simpler here. No pressures to speak of. Friendly natives. Foreign tastes and smells. An exoticness in the air that's hard to define. Whether it's your first trip, or you've been coming down for decades, it's hard to get over the sense of homecoming you get when the dry warm breeze first hits your face when you step off the plane.

If you're reading this, you've probably gotten serious about making it your home, or one of your homes. Congratulations. There are worse places to hang your hat. I've been down here for years, and it feels like I just got here. Time passes differently in Baja, that's one of the inexplicably mysterious and alluring things about the place.

So where do you start?

First, you'll need to hook up with a good realtor who can locate candidate lots for you to look at. Alternatively, you can browse through any of the dozen or so real estate periodicals, or go directly to one of the developments peppering the landscape and see what their inventory looks like.

However you manage your hunt for the ideal lot, you'll need to take some time to consider important aspects of the offerings before you sign on the dotted line. Obviously, the first is location. What are your search criteria? What are your hot buttons? Do you want to be close to Cabo's restaurants and nightlife, or do you favor something a bit more tranquil by San Jose? Perhaps you want an older Baja feel, and are thinking of Los Barriles or La

1

Ribera, or are interested in being a bit off the beaten path and want the East Cape's solitude as your backdrop?

As you weigh the possibilities, consider each area's positives and negatives. Are you older, or do you plan to have older relatives living with you or staying for long periods of time? Do you need to be close to health care? Are you concerned about the security of remote locations or areas outside of gated, guarded communities? Do you like to golf, and would being near or on a golf course have appeal?

There are any number of criteria that can make an area your target. Often, price is an issue. So this is my first bit of advice: Cabo is an efficient market, for the most part, and there are no windfall deals any more. You tend to get what you pay for. Oceanfront commands a huge and deserved premium. So does being in one of the marquis communities that have sprung up over the last five years or so. Between 2003 and 2008, property values roughly tripled in the better areas, and as the region became more developed most of the hidden gems got snapped up. Even the East Cape and the Pacific side, with no power or water, took off in price, and never looked back. People figured out that the Cabo area was a secure investment choice, and an appealing place to live. The advent of the *Fideicomiso*, which is a Mexican land trust that allows a foreigner to be its beneficiary, transformed the ownership proposition and enabled gringos to buy land without fear of many of the games that had plagued Baja in the past. Third party escrow services came into town, as did title insurance companies, and suddenly what was a speculative and risky deal a decade ago became well defined and relatively safe.

So here's my second bit of advice: If you're going to buy, get title insurance, and make sure all verbal assurances are spelled out in writing. This is for your protection. You don't want to discover at the end of the day that you bought a decade-long title dispute, so pay up and do it correctly. Trust me, it isn't worth the money you'd save on title insurance if something goes bad and you don't have it. Think of it as a seatbelt – you hope you'll never need it, but are glad for it if something unexpected happens.

Those are the only caveats I have for the actual purchase part of the enterprise. There are many fine and professional realtors in town who can explain far better than I the procedure for buying a lot, so I won't waste ink duplicating their knowledge base. Instead, let's focus on qualities you need to consider when evaluating lots.

View

Probably the most important for me, after location, is view. Here, as in the United States, view is king, and will command more the better it is. MSN had a great article in the summer of 2008 discussing the premium that an ocean view carries. Oftentimes, view lots are fifty percent to double or more the value of similar lots with no view. That's a lot of cheddar. So when you go out lot shopping, make sure you completely understand what kind of view you'll have. Don't believe anything you're told – you'll need to see a plot map of the lot to determine where a house can sit, and you'll also want to get plot maps with elevations (if possible) of all lots in your view corridor. That will tell you what, once everyone builds, you'll be looking at.

I spend a ton of time studying lot maps for clients, as it isn't always obvious what you can do with a lot. I also spend a great deal of time walking a lot before I design anything, but that's long after the lot's bought.

Before you plunk down any change, you need to completely understand what you're buying. A great view today may be a blocked view tomorrow. The neighboring lot maps will clear that up. You'd be surprised how few people actually take this step before writing an offer, only to discover the hard way down the road that what they thought they were getting is different than what they got.

And it isn't just the surrounding lots you need to consider. If there's land that's outside the development you're evaluating, you'll need to predict the worst in terms of what will be built on the land between you and the view. Just envision the lot with a four story condo built on the nub of a hill between it and the ocean, and you'll get my drift.

But for the purposes of this book, let's hypothesize a lot in a planned community, where only the other lots in the community are in the way. Planned communities are generally pretty good about supplying the neighboring lot plans. They're also pretty good about advising, via their CC&Rs, what level everyone can build to. Which brings me to the next item you'll have to get, and study, before you write any checks – the CC&Rs, assuming there are any.

CC&Rs and Buildable Elevations

CC&Rs define a host of criteria for building in a community. They're created by the developer, and reflect conditions that owners must follow in order to build. Everything from setbacks, to home size, to roof pitch and type, to style of home, to buildable elevation, will be laid out in unambiguous terms. Most of the better communities have well-articulated CC&Rs, and you absolutely have to invest some time in reading them and becoming an expert on the relevant sections before you write an offer. If you're unsure what the CC&Rs mean or how they limit you, ask an expert. And with all due respect to sales guys, I don't mean ask the sales guy and believe whatever he says. I mean ask a designer, builder, or architect. The problem with verbal assurances from sales folk and developers is that the assurances are verbal, and have no legal weight. You need definitives before you buy.

And don't assume. Assuming is dangerous. I've talked to folks who assumed all kinds of crazy things about what CC&Rs say, when they clearly don't say anything like what was assumed. One example is pad level. In a famous community in SJ, several of the residents built their homes at natural ground level, or below their allowed pad level, because they assumed that neighbors couldn't build above the allowed pad level. It came as a nasty surprise to them when they discovered that their interpretation was in error (although I would have thought their architects would have explained things to them – another erroneous assumption….see what I mean about assuming?) and their neighbors could and did build higher than their pad level starting point.

The problem was the assumption that the pad level was an absolute limit to the ground floor elevation. Not so. A pad level is indeed a starting elevation, but only for the purpose of calculating the maximum elevation a home can be built to, using the guidelines in the CC&Rs. In this case, for a two-story home, the limitation was 10 meters above the pad level.

Now follow along with some back-of-the-napkin math. Each story of a home will run about 4 meters or so, for a two-story structure. If we use that 4 meter per floor rule of thumb, we get 8 meters of structure. But wait, the CC&Rs allow 10…

The missing 2 meters can be added to the bottom elevation, to raise the overall home up and provide views that wouldn't be available if you started the build from the allowed pad level. A great idea, as in this community, the homes that chose this route wound up with breathtaking ocean and beach views from both floors, as opposed to views of the neighbor's house from the ground floor (had they not raised the home).

You can imagine how the neighbors felt when these homes went in. They felt cheated, and were annoyed at the "towering" homes. The truth was that they didn't do the homework to understand what they could have built on their lots, and they made assumptions that were incorrect – however knowing the truth didn't change their displeasure. At the end of the day, though, there was nothing to do and nobody to blame, as the taller homes had simply run the calculations and decided to optimize their views – as allowed in the CC&Rs.

Here's another germane story. A buddy of mine had me design a home for him on a lot that was articulated in the CC&Rs as a single story lot, meaning that it could only be built 4 meters above the allowed pad level (that community limits each story to 4 meters). The lot he was considering had been rejected by many buyers, as even though it had stellar views, due to the lot size you could only get maybe a twenty-five hundred foot single story home onto the lot, and it would have been oddly shaped (the lot was a radical pie slice shape, so single story would have been awkward, to say the least). He was deeply disappointed, as the seller's realtor confirmed for him that it was indeed only capable of supporting a single story home of rather modest proportions – not what he had in mind for his dream home.

I went out, checked it out, and then sat down and read the CC&Rs and looked at the lot maps. What I figured out, that had escaped all the other potential buyers, was that indeed you could only build 4 meters above the articulated elevation for the pad – a single story. But nothing limited you in terms of building down. This lot was an uphill slope, and the pad level was about 5 meters above the street, which was at the base of the lot. Everyone had just assumed that you'd have to put a garage down, then build the house on the bluff. What I did was ran the numbers, and calculated that you could instead fit five thousand feet of two story home on the same twenty-five hundred foot footprint (two stories), with a garage at a third level a bit below the street level. Presto, different kind of home, and different approach to the same piece of dirt. My friend bought the lot, I designed the home, and he embarked on building a completely different place than anyone had envisioned.

The takeaway is that CC&Rs are your friend, and your limiting factor, when you buy your lot. They're the user's manual. You need to devote a couple hours to mastering the relevant information so you can make an intelligent purchasing decision.

Slope

As in the prior story, slope plays a huge role in the desirability of a lot. It also plays a significant part in the economics of building, as excavation or landfill can be a massive cost on "difficult" lots. Slope can be deceptive, as a flat lot can lull a complacent designer into just slapping a home on the natural ground level, when raising the pad might make a huge difference in the resulting view. As with everything else, the ramifications of slope aren't as easy to recognize as you might think.

To put things into perspective, a larger lot with a "gentle" couple of meter downward slope could wind up costing hundreds of thousands of dollars for landfill. Even as the seller describes it as "almost flat", once you clear the lot and start thinking in terms of construction, you might get sticker shock from what it costs to bring that "almost flat" lot to a buildable state.

My advice is that if you don't have an engineering degree, and can't calculate the rough number of cubic meters of dirt that will be required to create a platform, you should get help. And I don't mean a guess from the selling agent. Again, that will be verbal, and largely meaningless, unless he *does* have an engineering degree and is up to speed on the cost in that development for landfill, compaction, etc. If you're serious about buying a lot, spend a couple bucks and get an expert out to do real calculations.

One important caveat: Once a designer gets involved and you start on a plan, you may discover that you'd be best served to raise the pad even more than what the baseline allowed is. In that case, your costs will obviously be higher.

And on uphill lots, you'll find that excavation isn't free, and you need to factor it into your calculations. The wild card there is what's under the brush and dirt – sometimes it's solid rock, which can require months to cut away using large earthmoving gear. One solution would be to get an American geologist out to do some soil samples so you have a decent idea what you're buying. A cheaper and almost as good solution is to talk to others who have built in the same area on uphill lots, and find out what they went through. You'll quickly get a feel for what you're looking at.

My advice is to think of the total lot price as the cost of the lot, *plus* the cost to fill it or excavate it. So a $250,000 lot that requires roughly a $150,000 to fill it, is in reality a $400,000 lot. If you understand that, and it still fits in your target budget range, then you should be comparing it to other $400,000 total cost lots, not other $250,000 lots. It's the final cost that you care about, not the component parts.

Size

A fairly obvious way of determining the value of a lot is size. Clearly, size matters. When you see meters used, just multiply by 10.764. So a 1000 meter lot would be 10,764 square feet.

But beyond size, you also need to take into consideration the allowable buildable plot area. In planned communities, this can significantly reduce the amount of land available to build upon, the idea being that you want room between your house and your neighbor's. So you want to consider the size of the buildable area before you plunk down cash – will it work for the type of place you envision?

A lot of folks come to Baja and use rules of thumb that would be comfortable back home, and wind up with a lot that's way too small for their ultimate liking. Certainly, some of the older communities here have very small lots, as in 400 meters – and while you can build a home on a postage stamp sized lot, oftentimes that doesn't yield an end result that clients are happy with. Better to go a bit larger than you think you'll need, than to shoehorn a project into a small lot.

The flip side of that's that larger lots can pose significant challenges in terms of upkeep and expense. Landscaping can cost an arm and a leg for a 2200 meter lot, which is the average size in some marquis communities' ritzier sections. And when you're talking about not just maintaining a lot that size, but also potentially having to level it with landfill, you can have a significantly more expensive proposition than you might have bargained for. Take some time to carefully consider what you're getting into before you buy – sometimes the cost of acquisition is a fraction of what the total freight will be.

Once you have a decent idea as to what the combination of the lot plus the landfill will cost, you can move to retaining walls. You don't need to be super granular and to-the-penny at this point, just in the ballpark. The goal is to plug in all the numbers, and then divide the sum of all the parts by the number of meters. That's your per-meter true lot cost.

Retaining Walls

Virtually all lots that aren't completely flat will require some sort of retention system to hold the dirt in, or keep the dirt out. This is why taking some time to investigate the amount of landfill required (or amount you need to excavate and remove) is key, as mentioned before. Once you understand how much dirt you'll need, you can ask an architect or engineer to roughly calculate the retaining walls needed to hold the dirt in place. This gets complicated, of course, as often the retaining walls are part of the home design, so if no design has been drawn, it's all just a guess based on very rough assumptions. Still, you should be able to get at least a coarse idea of what you'll need.

Again, retaining walls can be a relatively trivial expense, or they can be more than the cost of the lot. Best to know which before you buy.

As a rough rule of thumb, downhill slope lots are going to need fairly significant retaining walls to keep your home from sliding down the hill. The steeper the slope, the more complex the likely network of walls needed.

For instance, I looked at a lot on a hilltop for a broker, where we calculated that it would take about twelve stories of retaining wall structure to support a platform for a 3500 sqaure foot house. No exaggeration. Cost would be closer to a million dollars than a hundred grand just for the walls and dirt. When you build that sort of structure, it can take a year or more, and is a major project. This one was even more complicated as the CC&Rs required that the entire thing be surfaced with natural stone.

As readers of my columns know, dirt isn't free, and neither is rock. A few years ago, dirt actually increased in price by over fifty percent, as did rock. Now, you might think that dirt is free, and you would be partially right – some dirt is in fact free, but trucking dirt isn't. Same for rock. The ground may be littered with it, but when you need a dozen square meters of it loaded and brought to your site, you'll discover that it's almost as pricey as rare marble. Which is another reason you want to study your CC&Rs. Some communities require many, or all, retaining walls to be surfaced with stone. Those are way more expensive walls than mortar and paint walls.

At the end of the day, the two big adders for your lot will be landfill (and/or excavation), and walls. Best to get an idea of what you're looking at before you dive into the water, as otherwise you could be faced with owning a lot you can't afford to build on. I've seen that happen before, and it ain't pretty.

Topography, Water & Power, *SEMARNAT*

Always get a third party topography study on your lot. Always. There are no exceptions to this rule, and it's as seminal to basic building as mortar and rebar.

Don't trust the developer's topo, as often the lots were surveyed very quickly, and developer topos have been known to be off. That's a huge deal when you're calculating landfill to bring your platform height to the suggested level to build. It's your responsibility as the owner of the lot to get a topo done so you understand what your true lot surface looks like. The developer's topo is just a guide.

I've actually built homes in communities where the developer's topo was off by at least a meter, as the topo had been done before they put in roads, and the levels were approximations. I've also built homes where the neighbors skipped the step of getting their own third party topo, with sometimes disastrous results.

Imagine that you think you're building from a level of say, eight meters above sea level, and in fact you're only building from seven (due to reliance on the community topo, that's off by a meter). Your neighbor gets a topo done, and he builds from true eight, creating a retaining wall problem for you – the rule is generally if you excavate or build below the pad level you're allowed, you need to provide retention to keep the dirt that *you* made into a problem from sliding into your lot. If you raise your lot above the pad level, then you need to handle the wall for anything above pad level. In both cases, you created the problem, so it's to keep your lot from either filling up with dirt, or eroding into the neighbor's yard, that walls are required. But if the neighbor builds below the pad level and you raise yours, you're really only on the hook for the portion that's above the pad level – again, they chose to build below it, so that wall is on them.

A topo is worth every penny you spend on it, and it's a requisite. It can avert disaster, and provide a fingerprint of what you're buying. Consider it mandatory. If you're thinking of buying a lot, have that be one of the "subject to" conditions of the purchase: Subject to your obtaining and approving a topo.

So now onto other important items to consider – power and water.

Most Cabo and San Jose developments have both power, and city water. That's pretty much a given, until you leave the metro areas, at which point you should take nothing for granted. Many East Cape developments and lots do not have any water, or power. That isn't necessarily the end of the world, but it's kind of important to understand going in.

I've built projects in the East Cape where the only water available was from a shared line coming from a private well. If the line broke due to construction, or a cow trampling it and splitting the plastic, everyone was out of luck until the leak was discovered and fixed. I've also seen areas where the agents glibly tell purchasers that they might want to consider getting a well permit. Ha. Might as well try to get a permit to land a 747 on a dirt airstrip. Well permits used to be relatively simple items to get, but for single family residences, it's a long uphill battle. You might as well resign yourself to getting water trucked in once every month or so – not the worst thing to have to do, but still, not as convenient as being on city water.

And then there's the question of power. Again, verify that the lot actually has power lines running onto it, and that others in the area have power. If not, regardless of what's "projected" or "planned" it's a lot with no power.

I've also done projects requiring solar as the exclusive method of powering the home. It's actually not a bad deal, as you never have to worry about blackouts, but the cost going in can be high. And if you're going to run AC, you have to plan to have a backup generator, usually a large one. Solar homes, "Off the grid", are not as rare as you might think, however they require completely different planning than conventional homes.

Speaking of power, let's turn back to the good old CC&Rs. If you're looking at a community with CC&Rs, make sure you pay special attention to whether or not they bar the use of solar panels. Some of the more exclusive ones do exactly that, which you need to understand should you be considering things like solar heating for your pool. Just another checklist item to understand, however better to know this before inking the deal, rather than after.

And while we're on the topic of utilities, also find out whether there's city sewage, or if you'll require a sewage treatment plant of your own. One community on the corridor tells prospective buyers that there's city sewage, but after you buy, you discover that the pipes have never been hooked up to the city pipe, thus you still require a treatment plant. Read the CC&Rs, as they should call out how sewage needs to be handled. Putting in a plant isn't a big a deal, but it's yet another potential expense you would be better advised knowing in advance of buying anything.

SEMARNAT

If you're considering buying an oceanfront lot, or a lot outside of an established community, you'll need to take into account *SEMARNAT* – the ecological and maritime area protection agency whose permission you'll need to obtain before you build.

SEMARNAT will generally require an Environmental Impact Study/ Report before it will grant you permission to build – not an inexpensive proposition. And as with many things in Mexico, also not something that takes place quickly.

You'll need to hire an authorized examiner to generate the study, usually after you have blueprints done. The examiner will study the lot and the surrounding area to ensure that you won't be disrupting any of the ecosystem with your project. He will gather his findings into a report, which needs to be submitted to *SEMARNAT* along with a request for the permit, and a slug of pesos. They'll study it for around three months, and usually it will be approved after that time. It can take longer, but don't expect it to happen any faster. Back in the good old days, a singly family home could expect to get a waiver to the environmental study requirement, however those days are gone. Pretty much all of them now require a permit, unless the developer obtained a blanket one for the community when the development was created. Ask about this.

SEMARNAT also deals with the Federal Maritime Zone – the area between beach lots, and the ocean. There's a strip of beach after the lot ends, on the ocean side of the lot, that's part of this zone, the idea being that it's public property. But it can get more complicated. There's also what's called a concession, which is the right to use this area in front of your lot – if someone wants to get it, and set up a jet ski stand in front of your oceanfront abode, they can, unless you obtain the rights. So my advice is that when you're looking at oceanfront property, you have a serious discussion with the realtor about simultaneously obtaining the concession, or you run the risk of having a living nightmare down the road.

This concludes the lot portion of the guide. See the following checklist for a quick refresher, and use it when you go shopping to avoid headaches.

Checklist

- Location. Access to health care, required services

- Title Insurance.

- View. Neighboring or community lot map with elevations. Lot plan with elevations.

- CC&Rs. Building elevation limitations, setbacks, design style.

- Slope. Landfill estimate. Excavation estimate.

- Size. Buildable area. Size make sense? Cost per meter reasonable?

- Retaining Walls. Estimate of number and cost. CC&R requirements for appearance.

- Topography Study. Get one, or make purchase subject to. Verify Utilities. Verify *Semarnat* requirement if any, and if oceanfront, also concession issue.

CHAPTER 2 – DESIGN SELECTION

You have your lot, and you want to build a house. So now what? How to go about it, and get the best possible outcome? Where do you even start?

I advise my clients to start at the beginning, and treat the project much like a class in school. Probably the most important thing one can do in school to be the most successful comes down to a simple word: Homework.

First thing I try to get my clients to do is spend a lot of time standing on their lot, getting to know every inch of it. The land tends to dictate the design, to a great extent, or at least it should. All lots are different, all terrain is different, and yours is unique. You're going to wind up spending a lot of time through the building process watching the home go up, and you'll likely spend hundreds of hours walking through it in different stages, so might as well start by spending some serious time on the raw land, considering what would look best there.

While you're making pilgrimages to the lot, you should look at homes in the area, and think about what style you like. I actually encourage my clients to try to go through as many homes as possible, and to take pictures of as many features as they can so as to memorialize their likes and "must haves." But before you start debating the merits of bidets or under-counter refrigeration, you need to get into the car, and start looking at homes.

Does your taste run to the Mediterranean villa, with an approach that would be at home on the Spanish coast? I do a good deal of work in this style, and it can lend itself to spectacular results. Look at the newer hill section of Palmilla, or Cabo Del Sol for typical examples. Columns, arches, *teja* roof tile, copious exterior cantera, brick domes, arched windows, wood-look window frames, classical lines.

Or are you more the Hacienda kind of person? More of a courtyard-based style, with rustic touches, exterior wood, elaborate stonework, dark carpentry, intricate ironwork, something that looks more at home in communities like Querencia or some sections of Puerto Los Cabos? This is a very popular look around Cabo, and I've drawn and built quite a few homes in the vein, with nice results.

Or are you more of a contemporary person, favoring the clean lines and geometric precision of the Mexican masters whose work has made the approach wildly popular? This is the sort of thing that Baja architects like Jacinto Avalos have made world famous. In the style of Louis Barragan and Ricardo Legorreta, the design philosophy is very symmetrical – it features squares or grids, often uses tall, thin "sunset windows", and eschews exterior flourishes that the style considers gratuitous or unnecessary. This is one of my personal favorite approaches, as it can offer tremendous impact using minimalist sensibility.

Perhaps you resonate with what I call "Ranch Santa Fe" – a sort of hybrid of the Hacienda approach, and more of the faux-Tuscan theme that one can find populating the hills of Rancho Santa Fe, California? This style will often have towers, more square than rounded lines, and will blend extensive use of exterior cantera with more modern California design flourishes. It's a little bit Mexico, a little bit California, and you can find many good examples in communities like Punta Ballena.

Or do you fancy a mission style place, something that looks like it was built three hundred years ago, and is part of the legacy of the original Spanish missionaries who conquered and developed Mexico? These can be a lot of fun to draw, and typically will feature rounded, bell tower entrances, oversized doors, heavier approaches to spaces, and very rustic flooring and wall treatments.

Whatever your flavor, you should spend at least one trip driving around the various communities, and looking at what others have chosen to build. What will happen is that you'll be exposed to many different takes on the Baja lifestyle, which in turn will get the juices flowing and force you to narrow down which approach most resonates with your taste. Take pictures. Lots and lots of pictures. As you go through those after the trip, what will inevitably happen is that you'll find yourself going back to one or two homes as the best example of "it" you can find.

Photos will come in handy when you get into the actual design process. Reason being is that words are ambiguous, and can mean different things to different people. But photos eliminate much of the guesswork. You may think you're being very clear when you describe to your designer what you want, but you'll be surprised by how many folks use completely different vocabularies to describe the same sorts of things. That can create nightmares and false starts in the design process.

When considering what style you favor, don't be too quick to answer, and take your time looking at different examples of the breeds before you make a final choice. One client of mine came to town, and was very specific that the sort of home he had in mind was a southwestern Mexican style that can be seen in some of the tract corridor developments. No problem, easy enough to draw. But as we went around and looked at lots, and inevitably walked through homes in the communities we were considering, the big surprise was when we walked through a home being built on the beach in the East Cape. This home's design approach was pure Barragan contemporary styling, through and through.

The client stopped when we finished the little walk through, and declared, "This is what I was trying to explain I want. Clean lines, large spaces, simple, pure design approach with minimal flourishes. Let the design do the talking."

Again, this illustrates the shortcoming of using words to describe what one envisions. Your mind's eye description of "southwestern" or "hacienda" may be completely different than your designer's idea of "southwestern" or "hacienda". You may be thinking about a mission-style home that would be perfect in Cabo Del Sol, and your designer may be thinking about something more akin to the latest wave of pseudo-hacienda styling that can be seen around Punta Ballena.

Getting a feel for exactly what you're trying to achieve before you walk through the door of a design firm can greatly increase the productivity of the design phase, and I strongly encourage my clients, if they can, to find a house that closely reflects the design approach they want, and take photos. That eliminates the aforementioned dreaded ambiguity, as ambiguity in the design phase can translate into frustration with the finished product.

Size, Features & Quality

Size matters. In Baja, more than anywhere else, space is appreciated, and is sought after by most coming to the area. The region lends itself to indoor/outdoor living, and spacious approaches are absolutely the most popular.

A common question for those new to the region is, "What's the right size home for Baja?" That depends on a number of factors: Neighborhood, intended use, desired amenities, budget, lot size and configuration.

You need to consider where you're building before you make any size decisions. If your target community is 5000 to 9000 foot homes, you're making a big mistake building 3000. And if you're neighborhood is mostly 2500 foot homes, don't build your Parthenon there.

"Build appropriately for the community" is always my counsel. So my answer to the question, "How big is the right size?" is, "Depends upon where."

Of course, it also depends on why you're building; to use as your residence, to lease as a vacation rental, or to sell as an investment vehicle? I design differently depending upon intended use. You should too. If as a rental or spec home/investment, consider the most popular requisites over personal taste/desires. If as a residence, don't try to anticipate everyone else's likes and dislikes – design what you want to live in. How many times in your life will you get to completely define your environment, down to the last detail?

I've designed dozens of homes in a wide variety of styles in Baja, and I've found that some key elements tend to be more desirable than others. As you consider "must have" features and desired flourishes, you might want to peruse my short list of thoughts, based upon what seem to be the most popular criteria. In no particular order:

1) Single story master entertainment/living areas are very, very popular. Even in multi-story, owners typically want to stay on one level.

Master bedroom and bath, living/dining/kitchen, garage and outdoor entertainment area on the same level is a big positive. Especially as folks age, the desire to have everything on one floor, with a minimum or complete absence of steps, moves to the forefront of design imperatives. Simply put, steps are a slip and fall waiting to happen. Anyone that has aged relatives, or is of a certain age themselves, will understand why it's best to avoid designs that feature stairs or steps for the primary area. That can fly in the face of many design approaches you'll see around town, where creating "interesting" areas – sunken dining rooms requiring several steps down, courtyards with ledged steps down to the main area, spiral staircases to provide design flair – seems to be far more important than creating livable floor plans.

I can totally understand and appreciate richly evolved multi-level approaches to single levels. I admire them tremendously, and can draw 'em with the best of them. I just choose not to very often, as they don't really work for the majority of older clients, especially if disabilities are looming on the horizon. I tend to use a simple rhetorical tool to figure out if the primary areas are best served as multi-level. I ask questions like, "What will happen the first time your drunken uncle or friend misses one of those steps on the way from the bathroom, or to the kitchen?"

Around Cabo, it's not unusual to find homes with lots of steps, even when they're single level homes. Steps up or down to a dining room. Steps from an entry to a foyer, and then further down to a living area. Spiral designed stairways that make one dizzy when one looks at them. Curved stairways from one area to another, wholly lacking any handrails.

That affords a sense of movement in the floor plan, and is terribly interesting architecturally, however if you're over sixty, it's a disaster in the making. Steps equate to opportunities to hit the ground hard – and with an older body and a stone floor, that can be a first and last time event.

One of my clients, a prominent physician, summed it up best when he popped out with an interesting statistic. Namely, that the average life expectancy of an older person (think over seventy-five or so) who falls and breaks their hip – the most common injury from slip and falls – is eighteen months from the time of the accident.

Now, that doesn't mean that all stairs are bad. Sometimes they're unavoidable. I will say that many of my clients are adamant that they don't want stairs in their home, for exactly that reason, as well as just for general comfort. And I've done several designs that are heavily focused on wheelchair accessibility for all the areas, as one of the unfortunate realities of old age can be restricted mobility. It's one of the reasons I try to stick with smooth pool deck area material, like cantera tile, rather than rock. Not only is rock impractical when using a walker or any sort of device designed to assist in stability, but it also gets hot enough to light a cigarette on during the summer months – so I try to stick to materials that are practical for older guests or inhabitants to get around.

Everyone has a parent or relative who is older, and many of my clients are of a certain age, and I can tell you flat out these sorts of things are a concern. They also make a huge difference on resale. Nobody wants someone's design experiment if it requires a trapeze and a gymnastics background to navigate safely.

Basically, if a design features multiple slip and fall opportunities, or ignores the realities of aging like walkers, wheelchairs, and broken hips, I tend to say, "Pass."

Obviously, this doesn't apply to multi-story homes, as you'll inevitably need stairs to get from point A to point B, but even then I try to eliminate stairs to the extent I can on each level. I also argue for elevators if the budget will allow, as the cost has come down to where an elevator isn't wildly extravagant any more, and nicely solves the question of how to get up and down once the ravages of time have worked their magic on the body. An elevator is also a big plus for resale, as it opens the door for more buyers on multi-story structures.

2) Full size two-car garage is a must. Storage in the garage is also a must. Golf cart parking is also a consideration in communities where golf courses are part of the mix. Three-car is usually overkill for all but the largest homes, or in rural areas with lots of space.

3) A boat and/or RV garage is a big plus in those rural areas.

4) Maid's quarters are a nice addition, even though most will never have a live-in maid. That's where you park rowdy siblings or in-laws.

5) View is king. Anything you can do to maximize the view, do it.

6) Pantries are good. Bars are good. Outdoor BBQ's are better left to movable devices, on spec homes.

7) Bigger/wider is better on stairs, kitchen islands, some doors, and most bathrooms.

8) An indoor/outdoor approach to living areas never goes out of style.

9) "Wow" entryways are good. You only get one shot at making a first impression. "Wow" entries into "Wow" great-rooms are even better.

10) A little running water in the design effects goes a long way.

11) Rock can be your friend on exteriors, but stay tasteful.

12) Domes are nice. *Campenarios* are nice, too. Arches and columns are also nice, as are disappearing walls, and intriguing and unexpected uses of textures and light.

13) Big without being cavernous can be tough to pull off. High ceilings are nice, but too high, and you have a bowling alley.

14) What sounds big at home, isn't in Baja. Homes are larger here. A good rule of thumb is add thirty percent to whatever you think is adequate. That might wind up being too small, but at least you'll be in the ballpark. People want space in retirement/dream homes, as well as in rentals – they want something special and better than what they have back home. It's still relatively inexpensive to build, so go larger, not smaller.

This last observation is critical. I can't tell you how many clients started out thinking they would be happy with 2800 feet, only to wind up at 4000 plus. That happens because as they walk through more homes here, and consider what they like best, the plans that feel the most hospitable tend to be larger.

Get clear on what you want to build before you start talking to anyone. Clarify the "must have" features you want. These typically include number of bedrooms and baths, general size of the home, stylistic influences, special rooms/features (wine cellar, home theater, family room, maid's quarters, gym, cage for the ex, etc.). You'll do better if you have a good outline before you approach a designer/architect.

The list of possible features you can include is virtually endless, however most add cost. So as with everything, you need to be careful in what you specify. Understand that every element in a home has a price, and that you can quickly run a budget into the ground by being unrealistic in terms of what you want. For instance, rooftop observation decks are very popular in some areas, however they increase cost. Iron railing costs. Built-in seating costs. Firepits costs. Stairs to the roof cost. Lighting costs. So while it can be a cheap way to increase livable space, it isn't a free way.

Same applies for all other features. You want fountains? Great idea. But they cost. Onyx walls? Ditto. Niches? Come with a cost. Crown molding? Love it. Costs some, though. Rag painting? Excellent, but not free. Fireplaces? Sure thing – at a cost.

The trick is to get everything you want and your budget will allow, without specifying so many features and frills that you push the budget out of sight. So consider what you want in your home, and make a list of, "Nice to haves" versus, "Gotta haves." At some point, that list will come into play should the building cost exceed your budget.

Speaking of budgets, recognize that there are really two things that will impact your build cost, beyond lot acquisition/landfill/retention: Size, and quality.

Size is obvious. The larger the footage, the more expensive.

But quality is a little harder to immediately grasp for many. Because there can be hundreds of dollars of cost difference per foot for homes that look, at first blush, much the same.

In later chapters we will cover elements that can impact your cost, including quality elements, however you should understand at the design stage that what you select as your model for what you want to achieve as a design, will hugely impact your cost. If the homes you prefer are homes that are of a style that use plenty of stone, cantera, exterior carpentry, and lavish ironwork to create their gestalt, that design decision will dictate a far more expensive-to-build design than one that's simpler in its finishes, and achieves its look more from the lines of the home.

Another way of saying this is that you should get clear on what quality of home you're considering building, as that will drive many design decisions. As an example, if you're dreaming of vaulted ceilings with impactful height, that design decision will result in a more expensive-to-execute design. If you want seven bathrooms, those will add significant cost. Every window costs something. Different types of windows cost more – as another example, arched windows are more expensive than square ones. So a design that requires arched windows and twelve foot ceilings will cost more to build than one with square windows and ten footers. You shouldn't drive yourself crazy over the minutiae, however just recognize that what you shoot for will determine what you wind up paying.

One thing I try to impart is that you need to be realistic when you pick a home type to model. If you select one that's on the beach in Puerto Los Cabos, or in Querencia or Punta Ballena, you're selecting from homes that are among the more expensive in Cabo. Nothing wrong with that, but you have to temper your desired design style with budget goals. It makes no sense to design a home that will cost two million to build, if your budget is less than half that.

Good designers will try to get a feel for what budget range their clients are shooting for before they sit down and draw, as what they draw will be driven not only by the requested style and features, but also by the budget they're working with. A lot of latitude can be achieved by clever design choices, however one can also wind up with an un-buildable plan if one isn't clear on the costs involved in different styles and choices.

As a rule, the more stone, cantera, moldings, exterior carpentry, and finish frills, the more the house is going to cost to build.

So as you go through the exercise of choosing a style for your home, you should also take the opportunity to get clear on what quality level you want on the finished product side.

- Are you looking for inexpensive, rustic quality? By that I mean ceramic or Saltillo tile floors, off-the-rack cabinets, pine doors, coarse finishes using inexpensive materials, and simple floor plans. At one time, that was the only quality most here could build, due to constraints on materials and skilled labor. That changed about seven years ago, as newer communities like Cabo Del Sol, and then Punta Ballena and its neighbors raised the bar. But rustic is still popular in rural areas, and in communities where quality isn't a stringent requirement.

- Or do you want mid-level quality, meaning the upper-tier of communities like Cabo Bello, or mid-level for Cresta Del Mar? This level has better finishes, with simple marble or travertine floors, granite counters, and more innovative floor plans. You won't see much, if any, cantera, exotic woods, or better stone, but the overall finish is good. Many $700,000 to $1.3 million dollar homes fall into this range.

- Or are you thinking high-end, which has several tiers of its own: High-end 1, which is the average Punta Ballena or upper-end of the Cresta Del Mar level, High-end 2, which is Palmilla, nicer Punta Ballena/Cabo Del Sol/Pedregal and Puerto Los Cabos level, or High-end 3, which is full blown opulent, sky's-the-limit showstopper, as in the finest homes in Pedregal and on the oceanfront in El Dorado, Puerto Los Cabos, and Punta Ballena?

Not surprisingly, each level commands an increased cost. Within each level, however, there's a range, and you should ask around to find out what it's costing to build in the areas you're choosing to model. That will tell you whether the design type and quality are in your budget range, or better left to shipping magnates and Wall Street tycoons.

View

View is probably the single most important, and often the most overlooked feature, a home can have. I've seen dozens of homes on lots that could have had breathtaking ocean views from every room limited to marginal views from only some of the rooms. I never understand that, as I'm a big view guy, and I try to get optimal views from every possible angle or room in anything I design.

Put simply, the more rooms with views, the more appeal a home will likely have. Views command premiums. You shell out a mint for an ocean view lot, doesn't it make more sense to optimize what you paid all the money for, rather than creating a design that limits views?

I've witnessed countless design efforts where most of the home's rooms have no or few views. I've seen oceanfront homes where only a great-room and the master have the oceanfront view. I've seen the typical Hacienda "U" design used time and time again where that approach limits the views from the home to just a couple of rooms (the U design looks like a U. The bottom of the U faces the view, and the rest of the rooms are centered around a courtyard. It's a design approach from mainland Mexico, where there are no views to speak of, thus creating an area of interest like a courtyard with a fountain is the best you can do. I think it borders on criminal to put that design onto a lot with ocean views, as it ensures that seventy percent of the areas won't have the million dollar view). I cringe when I see these efforts, as they'll wind up costing the clients big time when the day arrives to sell the home. What do you think will command a premium or sell faster? "Ocean Views From Every Room" or "Ocean Views From Master & Living Room"? It's pretty obvious to me. But it seems to escape many when they're thinking about a design.

To repeat. View is king, and should be subordinate to all other concerns. Not to say that crummy designs should be created solely to get better views, but by the same token, accepting a design that only affords views from a minor number of a home's areas is a bad bet.

We touched upon the importance of elevations in the prior chapter. The design is where all that elevation homework comes into play. Good designers will spend time at the lot, considering the flow of the terrain and the natural view corridors, and attempt to craft a design that harmoniously optimizes both. To do so, you need to understand what's going to be built on both sides of you, as well as between you and the view – generally around here, the ocean.

Some brief true stories that underscore the critical linkage between elevations and view. I got a call from one of the developers in town, whose customer had worked with a local architect for a year. The problem was that the developer, as well as the client, felt that they'd made a wrong turn somewhere in the process. When I met with them, the design they'd paid for was basically a box, where the primary view corridor completely missed the breathtaking views of Palmilla point, instead orienting the main rooms toward the houses across the way, and on the opposite end of the box, toward a golf course. It was a two-story affair, nothing intrinsically wrong with it, but completely unsuitable for the lot. There were no views to speak of from most of the place, which missed the whole point of what the client really wanted.

We discussed what they'd hoped to achieve, and it turns out that they bought off on the design because they'd been convinced by the architect that was the best the lot would support, and had forced themselves to grin and bear it.

So we took some time, reviewed the elevations, and then walked the lot…and nothing could have been further from the truth. After doing a sketch on the back of a napkin, they hired me to do a new design, and within ninety days I'd generated finished, stamped plans, with breathtaking Sea of Cortez views from every room. It was just a case of the wrong perspective, and the wrong architect. That was a happy ending, and a big mistake happily averted.

Another client came in with a three story design, garage down, and kitchen, dining and a couple bedrooms on the second floor, with the living area and two more bedrooms up. Barely five minutes into it, I sensed we had a real problem, which was a major letdown given they'd worked with a respected architect for *two years*. The husband was advising how all the stairways needed to be reinforced to accommodate a wheelchair elevator. Apparently the wife would be wheelchair-bound at some point, so he was thinking ahead. When I asked why they'd designed a three story home, where literally every meal required multiple levels to be tackled, they replied that they *had* to. Puzzled, I drilled down, and they explained how their lot wouldn't have an ocean view from the main/second floor anyway, and they'd become resigned to only having the view from the third level, so it didn't really matter that the main/second floor had the front door, a bathroom and the kitchen obstructing the view corridor – there would be no view there anyway. And they *had* to have the garage underneath that floor, as there was *no way* to get it at the same level as the main floor, hence three stories of stairs, and no view except from the front half of the top floor.

Wow. I took a few minutes to digest all that, and reviewed the topo and the elevations of the surrounding homes, and shook my head. "Hogwash. Raise the pad a few meters, and you get uninterrupted ocean views from both floors. And if you're clever, we can get your garage up to that new level, so no stairs on the main floor, where we can put the master suite, along with a great-room and kitchen and dining room and entertainment area. Presto, no stairs to fight, and no drama or excuses."

To make a long story short, after a rough start (I had to go to the lot with the couple with a ladder and a tape measure, as one of the pair thought I was lying about the levels and the view, and wanted to see it for herself), we did a whirlwind design turn, and had a completely new and different plan done in the four remaining days they were here. That was a tough one, as so much had been emotionally invested in the two year plan there was a lot of attachment to it, even though it scored poorly, and failed the most basic tests for them. I was extremely unpopular for most of that four days as I was the evil bearer of ugly news, although in the end they wound up ecstatic with their new plan, and we've since become good friends.

The point of all this is that elevations define your view, and you shouldn't take whatever comes out of the design machine for granted as being the last word or even the optimum one on elevations. I tend to design by looking at the maximum elevation your roof can be at, and then designing down. Sometimes concessions on ceiling height can get your ground floor up as much as a story higher than it would have been if you started designing from the ground up. So elevations are important, and you need to view your plan not only from the context of the elevations complying with the CC&Rs, but also from the context of the elevations maximizing your view opportunity.

I've been known to elevate a design's starting pad point by one, two, or three meters, to get views from every room. The cost to do so is generally minor compared to the impact a design with ocean views from every room commands. When you're thinking design, you should have the view in mind with each and every decision you make, as at the end of the day, the collection of rooms you build will be directly impacted by what they look at. Your designer should pay a great deal of attention to the surrounding pad levels to optimize your offering. So make that a key criteria.

Design Summary

There are any number of beautiful styles you can select from as the basis for your dream home. They range from the classic, all the way to the ultra-contemporary. The type of home, the size, and the finishes, will largely dictate the ultimate cost to build, so choosing all the above should be done with care. You can get a fair idea of what homes you favor will cost to build by asking around in the neighborhood those homes populate, or by asking reputable designers or builders, or knowledgeable real estate professionals. Understand, however, that costs move around year to year, generally up, so what it cost to build four years ago isn't going to do anything but depress you today. Try to educate yourself as to what it costs to build your quality goal *today.*

Design choices can play a large role in what a home winds up costing to build, so establishing a range for your designer to consider when drawing the plan is helpful to getting something that meets your budget objectives. Having said that, nothing is as important in the design equation as view, so that should be a critical factor when creating the plan.

Designing Vs. Building

When shopping for a designer, it's best to separate out the design phase from the building phase. The reason is that while they're related, they'll require different skill sets. While often the person designing your home *is* the best candidate to build it, that isn't always the case. Some really are best at a drafting table, while others are best in the physical world working with crews and maestros. Best to keep the selection of a designer separate from the selection of a builder, as you'll likely want competitive bids from similarly qualified builders. If you predetermine that the designer will also be the builder, you eliminated that prudent safeguard.

For clarification, there are two phases to go through after you buy your lot. They are:

1. *Designing* a home, and translating your vision into blueprints, which is the work of a design group. Designing can be a few weeks of intense work with someone you connect with, or months of back and forth defining every aspect of your home's look and feel. For some, design is intensely personal and creatively rewarding, for others, more akin to ordering a gourmet meal at a restaurant: they want it to look awesome and have great taste, but don't care much for the details of the preparation. Either approach, or anything in between, is valid. The only caveat is that you should use a local, as foreign architects/designers don't understand how to work with the indigenous materials, creating havoc in execution.

2. ***Building*** the design, where plans become reality. This is where theory and philosophy meet the Baja dirt. It's also where any number of mishaps can occur, due to poor communication, incompetence, or dishonesty. Builders, including architects who build, all work with materials choices, and labor choices. Unless you have a great deal of experience with Mexican materials and vendors, the wrong builder can take you to the cleaners, both in terms of costs, and quality. Labor's easier, presuming the crews are reasonably skilled. We'll leave discussion of materials and labor for later chapters.

Selecting a Designer

There are any number of skilled, conscientious, talented architects and designers working in Baja. There are also any number of not-so-great ones plying their trade here. As with all markets, there's a bell curve, where a very few remarkable talents sit at one end of the spectrum, a few truly dreadful ones sit at the opposite end, and the majority fall somewhere in the middle.

So how to go about selecting a designer who will deliver what you want?

Well, one way is to ask around to find out who designed homes you're impressed with, and which look like what you want. That's not a bad way to do it. Another way is to ask friends and neighbors who they used. Still another is to drive around your target community and see who is designing places you think match the style you're after.

Any and all can yield a decent field to choose from.

I tend to counsel potential clients to consider a number of elements when choosing a designer.

- *Similar Work.* Does the candidate have other designs that impress you, and reflect the type of place you hope to get? Are they in the same style as what you're shooting for? Some designers are gifted at contemporary themes, but don't do particularly well at more classical or rustic designs. Some are good at columns and arches, but are out of their element when attempting anything else. Some specialize in U shape haciendas, and have never seen a lot that doesn't cry out for exactly that. It's important to understand that you're hiring a designer for their expertise, and their taste. Does he/she have experience designing in the size range you're considering? Are his drawings detailed and artfully rendered, or do they more resemble stick drawings? The big item here is to choose someone with the skill and the taste to get your home right on the first go around, and past successes in the style you're after are a good indicator of your likely experience.

- *References.* Talk to people for whom the designer has done plans. Ask the clients how they liked the experience, whether they wound up with what they hoped, and what the time to create the drawings was. You should be able to talk to at least two fairly recent references in the same style and size you're considering.

- *Popularity.* Often, better designers are doing more work than less talented peers. Do you see their work around in the area you're considering building? Are they a "name"? Have you even heard of them?

- *Personality.* You're going to need to rely on your designer to create a plan that resonates with you. It helps if you bond with him, and get the sense that he "gets" you and what you're after. Does he seem easy to work with? Will he accept input and direction? Is he talented? Often, arrogance and a dismissive attitude can creep into the process once the designer has your business, so try to screen for that, unless being dictated to is something you find appealing. Baja is full of horror stories of architects who ignored all client requests, and generated pretty much whatever they felt like, scolding their clients when called onto the carpet. That's not a good place to wind up, and you shouldn't have to fight to get what you want from your designer.

- *Communication.* Do they speak the same language you do? Are you comfortable with their reaction time, and their communication style? When you call their references, ask how the communication process went, as often a designer will take weeks to get back in touch with a client, which can really get old as the design process wears on.

- *Delivery Time.* How long does it take to get a finished set of plans? How long does it take to get conceptual drawings or a floor plan? I generally take around four months to generate finished plans for most of my projects, however it isn't unusual to run across folks who have been working with their designer for two years and still don't have final drawings. Time to execute can vary considerably, so add this to your questions, and ask the references how long their plans took.

- *Price.* What's the cost for the design process, including finished blueprints stamped by the community design review board (if applicable)? How is the payment structured? A word of advice on this topic. Generally, you don't want to select attorneys, surgeons, or designers and builders, based upon price. And while a high price isn't a guarantee of greatness, a low price will generally be a reliable signal of something less. Again, I've seen a number of designs come into my company for building bids that need pretty fair rework just to be able to build them in the real world. Some can't even be inhabited as designed. Don't assume that all designers are equal in competence – they aren't. Price can often be your first warning that you're headed for a bleak start.

- *Location.* While it can be tempting to use a designer from back home, it's a lousy idea and one that generally fails. Without belaboring the myriad reasons why, I'll offer just a few obvious issues. First, we build with completely different materials and techniques than back in the States. Second, our wall thickness and other metrics are generally much different. Third, if an architect isn't local and can't walk the lot as many times as he needs to in order to get a competent design done, you're likely to wind up with something inferior. Additionally, you'll need a Mexican architect to review your plans and translate them into Spanish, and a Mexican engineer to do your structural plan, so you'll be spending considerable money on local talent anyway. If your designer is local, when you get to the building phase, if anything is awry at least you have the ability to make meaningful changes quickly. More on all this in the following chapter.

Using this list, you should be able to stay out of hot water. You don't want to start the process off with a horror story. There are numerous tales of nightmare design experiences, which inevitably go something like this: An architect is interviewed, and is impressive – charismatic, knowledgeable, able, enthusiastic about the project, and seemingly in sync with the client's wants. A deal's inked, money exchanged, and the client goes home. After a month or two, a preliminary drawing is generated, which may or may not reflect most (or any) of the desired features or style (if it doesn't, another month will go by before another drawing's done). Assuming it does reflect what the client wanted, two or three more months go by, after which the client starts asking where the plan is. They're usually told it's "two weeks away."

After another two to four weeks, the architect stops answering calls, and e-mails are curt one-liners saying "things are in process," and that the architect's tremendously busy, etc. Eventually, either a floor plan is produced, or the client returns to confront the architect, and is told that it's only a few weeks away…at which point the client flies home, and *then* the floor plan is produced (maybe).

That plan may have some, or absolutely none, of the things the client asked for. If it does (rarely), three or four more months go by, as small changes fly back and forth. If it doesn't, the architect will advise the client of why their desires are off-base, or explain that they lack the acumen to understand things the architect does, etc. At some point the client will get exhausted, and take whatever's produced, or will continue the struggle, which becomes a battle of wills, where the architect acts in the role of all-knowing parent, and the client is reduced to begging and threatening for what they want. At the end of eight months to two years, a plan is produced, oftentimes with considerable client dissatisfaction. It's accepted due to the process having worn the client down to where they're just happy it's over, and they're relieved to have gotten anything at all on paper.

If you think this is an exaggeration, you haven't talked to many folks who've been through the mill here. If anything, this can be the mild version.

The goal of this section is to keep you from having this experience, or winding up with a design that's a train wreck. Both happen routinely in Baja, and both can be avoided with some basic diligence. This chapter is your outline of how to avoid the biggest landmines in the design phase. Follow the guidance and you should wind up with a good design, in a reasonable timeframe, at a reasonable cost.

The final, and most important criteria when choosing a designer, is that the designer also has to have significant experience actually building homes. This is critical and cannot be underscored enough. The reason it's so important is that guys who build things in the real world understand innately what will work well in that real world, and bring that perspective to the design table. Harsh experience has taught them the value of automatically including or altering things to make a build easier, or less expensive.

An example might be on a two story build. An experienced designer who's built homes will automatically line up all the walls so that they "work" and support the walls above. He'll be thinking like a builder as he lays out the design – hmmm, if I move that wall over a foot, it will cost five thousand dollars less to build the house than if I leave it where it is. The tradeoff might be fifteen more square feet of space to build, but the advantage of having the walls line up saves five thousand dollars, resulting in a net savings even after factoring in the greater space. This is an automatic thing for me, as I sort of strive to design not just from the perspective of the best floor plan and aesthetic, but also from the perspective of someone who will likely have to build the house and wants to have the most sensible use of resources and cost. Same sorts of decisions automatically take place on single level designs: "If that wall lines up with that one and that one, we can use a single structural beam instead of multiples, saving on the build cost."

It's hard to quantify all that goes into a design, and even harder to quantify what's an optimum design. I can say that I've had to modify a number of blueprints from respected architects in order to pull tens of thousands of dollars out of the build cost, by doing exactly the sorts of things I just described. It's tedious work, as once a design is finished and stamped there's a sense of finality to it, however if it will save ten percent on the overall cost to build the home, I have to introduce it as an option. Many architects and designers here also build so this isn't necessarily an issue, however it's a very important question in the qualifying process – "How many homes have you yourself actually built as the builder, and can I see some of them and talk to the clients?"

Design Checklist

- Walk The Lot. Spend some time on your property, getting a sense of the place. You have already got the topographical survey and CC&Rs from Chapter 1, so use those to study the lot when you aren't here.

- Look Around. Get a feel for the alternative design styles. Find ones you like.

- Take Photos. When you find them, take snaps of them. They'll come in handy when you describe what you're after to your designer.

- Consider Appropriate Size. Bigger is generally better in Baja. Think thirty percent larger than what you originally conceived and you'll likely be closer to what you'll want by the end of the process. Build appropriately for the community.

- Determine Features. List the basics – bedrooms and baths, pool, etc. Then list the "must have" features versus the "nice to have" features.

- Educate your Eye. Quality varies from community to community, and from style to style. Try to get a feel for what quality you want to design and build, and ask around to determine if you can afford it.

- Views Are King. Make absolutely sure you understand the view possibilities of your lot, and make that a top priority in the design approach. Ensure that your designer is on board with that philosophy, and that it reflects his/her approach.

- Separate Design and Building. Choose the best designer for the job, and worry about builders once you have a plan to build.

- Qualify Designers. Use the punch-list – Similar Work, References, Popularity, Personality, Communication, Delivery Time, Price. Use a local designer, as otherwise you'll be playing with fire that few have had success with. Select a designer with germane building experience so you get an optimum design.

Chapter 3 – Blueprints & Materials

By this point, you've interviewed designers, and selected a qualified candidate using the guidelines in Chapter 2. You've familiarized yourself with your property, had a topographical study done and secured a copy of the CC&Rs, and you've done your homework on target design styles, as well as the size and the features you want. Armed with photos of the type of home you're after, you sign the contract and embark on the design journey.

One thing to remember going into this process is that your blueprint is you home's DNA. If it isn't on the plan, it won't make it into your house. You can try just assuming that nobody missed anything, or that your designer has identical ideas as you do, but I wouldn't trust that too much, as everyone can make different choices. The problem with being unclear, or having ambiguity in your building plan, is that if something isn't defined you don't really know what will be built. That isn't a great recipe for success.

Doing a plan the way I suggest you do it forces everyone to think through each area of their home. Some only do a cursory review, which is fine assuming they have faith in their designer's acumen. Others prefer to roll up their sleeves and immerse themselves in most of the details. There's no right or wrong approach, although the more conversant you are with your plan's contents, the more likely you are to get the house you want.

Design Agreement

A word about the design contract. It should specify a number of things, to ensure that you're protected, and that you receive everything you'll need to build your house.

First, you need a timeline articulated for delivery of conceptual drawings, and then, from approval of conceptuals, to delivery of finished blueprints. This can vary greatly from designer to designer, but generally you should be able to see something preliminary within two to four weeks. The following is a list of deliverables you need to see articulated in your agreement:

Conceptual Drawing including floorplan. Once approved by you, you'll need:

1. *Arquitectonic* floor blueprint, with interior and exterior floor levels

2. Roofing blueprint

3. Electrical plans

4. Hydraulic/plumbing plans

5. Foundation floor plan

6. Facades, including cross-sections

7. Landscaping plan

8. Overhead exterior plan

You should get all this in both machine readable format (on disk, generally as a set of .DWG files generated in AutoCad), as well as in hard copy on at least one set of complete plans. The plans should be in Spanish, as you'll require Spanish language plans to get homeowner's association approval, as well as your building permit.

Additionally, you'll need to get a structural plan, and a *memorio de calculo*, which is a list of every element included in building the home. These are created by an engineer, not the designer, as the structural calculations and such will need to be certified by a registered Baja engineer.

Once all this is finished, you'll need to get a stamp from your homeowner's association for the plans to have been accepted (assuming there's a homeowner's association where you intend to build). It's generally a good idea to make the final payment contingent upon getting that stamp, as often modifications to the plan will be required, and you don't want those to be an extra charge. The designer is responsible for presenting the design to that group, and interacting with them to a successful conclusion. Once it's stamped, the job is done, and it's time to shop for builders.

As far as payment goes, half upon contract signing, and half at delivery of final stamped plans is generally the norm. Architectural and design fees are subject to IVA, the value added tax that runs ten percent in Baja. Construction typically isn't subject to IVA if the contract is structured appropriately, as there's a special exclusion for single family residential construction in the tax code. But professional fees, like architectural or engineering fees, are subject to the tax. That should all be articulated in the agreement.

If you decide to make changes after the design is stamped, those will usually be subject to an additional charge, as the designer has moved on to other things, the work on your project finished upon receiving the stamp.

The Blueprint Process

So your contract is signed, and you're in the process of designing your dream home.

Out should come the topo, CC&Rs, your list of desired features and amenities, and the photos of homes you like.

You should spend time with your designer, giving him a sense of what your expectations are, and how you live. He's the lens through which the builder will see your reality, and that reality will only be as good as his understanding of your wishes. So spend as much time as it takes for him to "get" what it is you're trying to achieve. This is an important deal for you, and it's best to get it right the first time. The worst thing in the world is to see a house being built, and to realize halfway through that it doesn't actually reflect what you wanted. I've seen that happen, and it can be expensive and agonizing to try to make modifications once it's no longer lines on paper. At this stage, it's just ink, so you want to ensure that the plan winds up delivering everything you want in a home.

To that end, I'll give you some tips as to how to evaluate your plan as you go along, so that the design momentum remains even as you scrutinize the drawings to ensure you're getting what you want. Before you start, though, let's get clear on something. You're the ultimate judge of whether the plan delivers for you, and you're also the final line of defence. So you need to take time to study the plan, and get good at understanding what all the lines and marks mean. You can't really tell what the plan calls for if you can't read it, so you need to have periodic meetings or e-mail exchanges where you ask questions and clarify ambiguities. In short, you need to get involved in your plan, and spend time studying it, and learn what the plan articulates. Many don't do this, and they're left baffled and disappointed when they see their home come up out of the ground.

As an example, I've had several clients who came to me to get construction bids, and when they unfurled their plans, they seemed completely unfamiliar with what was represented. For instance, it's not uncommon to talk to folks who have finished plans, who aren't really sure how big their house is. Think I'm kidding? Think again. They usually explain that the architect never really answered the question definitively, which tells me that they didn't ask the question definitively. They got all kinds of varying numbers – size of total construction, size of construction including decks but omitting other areas, size of AC area. But they don't really understand what it is they've paid for.

I can't tell you the number of times I've seen a plan where the client thinks they have a 3800 squre foot house plan, but it turns out to be more like 4500. This is astonishing to me, and tells me that neither the architect, nor the client, did their job. The architect's job is to listen to the client and get the project as close to target as possible, but the client's job is to comprehend what they got, to understand what they're looking at when they look at their blueprint.

As you've probably gathered, a fair amount of my business involves looking at plans other firms have done, and bidding the build. Unfortunately, all too often I scrutinize a plan with a sense of dread. While it would be wonderful if all drawings were equal, all executions similarly adept, oftentimes what's on paper has little to do with what the client wanted. And believe me, it sucks to be the one to have to tell it like it is. After spending a year or two sweating over a design, the last thing anyone wants to hear is that they have a stinker. It's no way to win popularity contests.

When a client comes in asking for a building bid, before looking at the plan my first questions probe for what they're hoping to build – what kind of place do they want? What are the hot buttons? What's the style they're after, and what do they hope to avoid? Are there special considerations? How big a house?

Then I look at what they brought in. On a good day, it's a strong plan that reflects what they described. On a bad day, it's something else again.

Let me be the first to say that taste is subjective. One person loves Barragan, another wants arches and columns, another wants rustic Mexican hacienda. They're all good, equally valid styles, and there's no "bad" design. Or rather, there shouldn't be. Too often, what's been created has notable and conspicuous deficiencies, and I have to weigh being complimentary and bidding the job, versus telling the truth and trying to save the train before it runs off the tracks.

The main problem I encounter is that many don't know how to read a blueprint and interpret it. So they aren't sure what they're looking at. Most just trust that their professional designer was competent and got the strokes right. Often not true. And if it isn't caught at the blueprint stage, it's a construction disaster in the making.

What can happen is that building starts, and at about month number five, the client flies down, and with a sinking feeling, realizes that what's now in concrete, isn't what they thought it would be. And nobody warned them, or took the time to go through things and ensure they understood what they were getting. It was a leap of faith, which really shouldn't require a parachute, but often does. It's not that it's being built wrong, but rather that what was signed off on isn't what was wanted. That's a depressing day.

As another example, I've had very nice folks come into my office with plans, asking for bids to build their home, and who thought they'd finished with the design process. I've gotten pretty good at asking pointed questions and then listening to responses, so I asked them what they thought the plan represented. I asked before we even unrolled it, as that would help me gauge whether they had a finished product, or something else. The number one thing that came up was that they didn't want any steps anywhere in the house, due to their age, and some medical issues. That, and they wanted a very rustic, old hacienda look.

We unfurled the plan, and I spent a few minutes studying it. I noted that there were four stairs coming from the garage to the home. They told me that was impossible. Nope, the lines representing stairs, along with the elevation markers showing the change in elevation were pretty definitive. So the primary entrance and egress point would require constant navigation of stairs. Needless to say, that wasn't the only issue with the plan, but again, it told me that the designer didn't listen, and the client didn't know what the plan they'd paid for represented.

So how do you avoid this sort of nightmare? What are the kinds of things you really should be watching out for, when deciding on who should design your house?

First is transparency, or rather, lack thereof. As discussed previously, there are lots of folks walking around who have no idea how big their house is.

How can that be? Simple – the architect won't tell them, or won't give them their plans in a measurable format, or every quote they've gotten calls things differently. But the bottom line is that they can't tell you for sure how large their home actually is, under roof, including the garage. So you need to find someone who will answer your questions in a straightforward manner, and level with you, and tell you what you want to know. Sounds simple, but you'd be surprised.

Another quick story to underscore my point. I met a nice young couple a few months ago, across the street from one of my designs, who are finishing up building their house. They asked me in to get my opinion on some items they were worried about, and the first question I asked was, "How many square feet is this?" They couldn't tell me. Asked me how many feet I felt it was. That took me aback, as how do you know if you're getting taken to the cleaners, if you don't know how many square feet you're building? Their statement was that the builder never really told them in a comprehensible manner, and that the building quotes were always confusing and smudged together, so they just signed on with the designer's recommended builder "partner" when the price "seemed" reasonable.

Reasonable being a relative term, obviously, as I'm the kind of guy who believes it's reasonable to know how many gallons of gas went in your car before you pay whatever the *Pemex* guy wants. Imagine if he wouldn't tell you, or launched into some long-winded explanation of liquid gas versus vapors created by the gas….but never answered the question. Hard as it is to believe, I run into this more often than you'd think – a significant percentage of the people out there with a plan don't really know how to calculate what they have in a manner that's meaningful. That's a larcenous builder's dream come true, as the more opaque the process is to the client, the greater the chance to run amok with costs. So here's a suggestion. If your architect won't tell you how large your house is, run away.

Ditto for another situation I run across – the architect won't give the client their Autocad files, the DWG files that will allow someone other than that architect to bid the project in a meaningful way, or to measure the entire structure. What kills me in this scenario is that's the client's property. The client paid for it. They own it. And yet, time and time again, I hear that an architect will only give a client PDF files, or that it takes weeks or months to get the DWG files – all of it, pure hokum, as sending DWG files is as easy as pushing, "Send." Alarm bells and red flags should go off if this sounds like your experience. Again, run, don't walk, for the nearest exit.

Transparency is critical for having a relationship of trust. My motto is, "Trust, but verify." Without transparency, there can be no meaningful verification, thus no meaningful trust. Make sense?

The goal of this chapter is to arm you with enough tools so that this doesn't become your experience. By the time you're done with it, you should know enough to be able to embark on the blueprint process with confidence, secure that you can tell up from down, and good from bad.

Broad Strokes – Evaluating the Plan

When I do a conceptual design, at the start of the process, I try to get everyone to evaluate the drawing in a crude, "Weighing" manner – to see if it covers essential bases. I've found if you give people tools to analyze their project, it instills confidence, as it allows them to evaluate what they're about to build.

What do I mean? Well, I tend to view a design, at a very simple level, as a series of possible "scores", or values. Each room has two possible totals, 20 total points per room, with 1 to 10 possible points for size, and 1 to 10 possible points for view (10 being best). The house's score is the number of rooms, times 20 possible points per room. A four bedroom house with five bathrooms, kitchen, dining, and living room, would have 12 rooms times 20 points per room, for a total possible of 240 points.

Then you go around the house, room by room, and score them. A guest bedroom? Is it big enough for the home's scale, or small condo size? If the latter, score it less than 10. If cramped, even lower. And what does it look at? As discussed, I'm a view guy. You moved here for the scenery and weather. So what's the view? If the ocean, that's a 10. If a wall or driveway, that's a 1. Golf course? Maybe a 6 or a 7, depending upon your love of the game.

I'll make a statement now that couldn't be underscored more strongly: As a designer, you should try to get "10" views and "10" size in every room. Period. Most of the time that isn't feasible, but you should have it as your goal. View is everything, along with adequate space. Doesn't matter what the style of the architecture is – view is king, and space is an imperative.

It can be an eye-opener to watch people armed with this basic mechanism for design evaluation, really "see" their design for the first time. You'd be surprised at how many possible 200 scores turn in a 100 or lower. I've found this an invaluable tool for clients to use on my design proposals as well as on the work of others.

Obviously, what you want is a score at the higher end of the range, which basically will tell you that you have an appropriately sized home with good views from all available view areas.

This of course assumes that you agree that appropriately sized spaces, and good views, are imperatives in your dream home. I have yet to meet someone who doesn't believe that both are critical, however if you don't think this scoring system makes sense, skip it and use something else to gauge whether your plan is good or not. I haven't heard of anything better, so it's what I encourage folks to use.

Blueprint 101

Measure Twice, Cut Once

When you look at your floor-plan, you'll need to be looking at things critically. Particularly, you'll need to understand dimensions and measurements.

I'm so used to working with metric system units that it's second nature to me. I encourage you to try to get comfortable with the metric system, as it's the unit of measurement used in Mexico, and Mexico is where you'll be building. Most of the numbers discussed in this book will be in meters, so you sort of get used to it.

To start with, a meter is 3.28 feet. That means that there are roughly 30 centimeters to a foot. So 30 centimeters is a foot, 3 meters is roughly 10 feet.

When dealing with square meters, you simply multiply the square meters by 10.764. Thus, if you have 100 square meters of house, you would have 1076 square feet of house. For rough and fast mental calculation, use eleven and then back off a hair.

I tend to encourage my clients to download one of the free software packages available to read and measure .DWG files. There are a number available, and spending a few minutes to become proficient using one is a must if you're to study your plans in a meaningful manner. This also enables you to save a lot of time by seeing progress examples of the plan via e-mail, and allows you to study the plans at your own pace when convenient for you. Some like to work late at night, some like to do it while on a conference call with the designer. Whatever works for you, with this software tool you have total control over your plan, and you aren't stuck waiting to see something whenever you can make it down to Baja.

Once you have this tool, you can start looking at your spaces critically. Take a kitchen. You can measure the distances between the island and the counter, and confirm that it's adequate for you to work in (1.2 meters or 48 inches is my standard, with some preferring 1.5 meters or more). You can measure the width of windows. You can measure hallways, stairways, and the sizes of critical areas (I try to do halls a minimum of 1.4 meters, stairs a minimum of 1.2 meters, and bathroom depths a minimum of 1.65 meters). What you're after is a sense of whether the spaces are large enough to accommodate American adults with acceptable comfort.

Doorways are an area you need to consider carefully. Many designers here will just automatically plug in a 75 centimeter (or smaller) door on bathrooms. That's fine, but ADA (Americans with Disabilities Act) guidelines require a minimum of 90 centimeters for a wheelchair to clear. You need to consider whether a smaller door is really what you intended, had you been asked, and had all this been explained.

Most opt for a 90 centimeter door on at least a few of their bathrooms, as well as the powder room for the main areas, and for all bedrooms and entry doors (like the garage entry – main entries should be much larger). And you also need to consider door height. 2 meters is standard (7 foot), however 2.4 meters looks better for most designs (8 foot and change). I tend to encourage my clients to go with at least 8 foot doors on all the important areas that will be visible to folks at a cocktail party at their home, and if they want to save money, design in 7 footers on the non-public areas, like guest bathrooms or guest closets.

I'm not saying that you need to be an expert at every element of your design, but you should have a good idea how the spaces are laid out, and what the dimensions of those areas are. Again, it's way more productive to understand all that when it's still on paper, as opposed to when it's concrete and rebar. Changing things at that point can be very, very expensive, whereas questioning whether proportions are adequate while the home is still lines on paper is cheap.

To that end, you should also look at room size, and determine whether things are as you wish them. Get a tape measure, and walk off the areas in question. If a master bedroom is 5 meters, and your master at home is 6 meters, you're going to be disappointed if you don't increase the size to match what you're used to. If your guest bedrooms are 3.5 meters square, you may want to walk that out and consider how spacious the areas will be once a bed and dresser and other sundry elements are in the room. If your bathroom has 45 centimeters between the toilet and the wall it faces, ask yourself if anyone older than a seven year old will actually be able to use it. Use your head when looking at shower sizes – can an adult (or two) actually use it without feeling like they're on a boat or in a camper?

Don't assume your designer is going to know any of this, as these are more United States considerations than they are Mexican. Many working here are used to dealing with United States proportions, but many aren't, and you can't take for granted that your plan is adequately sized. Check it, and then recheck it. Think things through. Walk off distances and consider whether the spaces work for you. Take the time to get it right.

I have walked through more than a few homes built by name companies that have stairways that are less than 3 feet wide – inadequate for a heavy person to get up comfortably, not to mention anyone who is carrying a suitcase or groceries. And forget about two people passing on that stairway – it's an impossibility. And yet it made it off the drawing board and into the homes. I've stood in showers that you couldn't fit into or turn around in without hitting your elbows. I've squeezed into bathrooms where there are only a couple of feet between the edge of the vanity counter, and the facing wall – forget about using it comfortably if you aren't a Kenyan marathon runner.

These are all examples that are typical of what can go wrong here if you don't pay attention to your plan. Proportions are important. They'll define the experience of the home, and how it shows.

Elevations

One of the most critical things about your plan will be the elevations. These will define your floor and ceiling heights, as well as the feel of the house, not to mention the views. There are small markers on a floor plan that denote the elevations. That's also a good way to tell whether stairs have been introduced into the mix. If the elevations change, barring a slope, there's a step involved.

Elevations will also determine the feel of each room, as ceiling height will be determined by the roof max elevation, minus the roof tile and the thickness of the support structure – generally 30 centimeters for the support structure and 10 to 15 for the tile.

So what's a good height for ceilings? Well, in a great-room, I try to do a minimum of 10 feet (3 meters), with a preference for going higher – say, 11 (3.3 meters) or 12 feet (3.6 meters). For bedrooms, 9 1/2 feet (2.8 meters) to 10 feet (3 meters) is usually sufficient, with the exception of the master, which can be higher.

On single story, you have more flexibility than on multi-story. But the biggest factor determining the optimum height is really the finished elevation of the house – the highest point the roof will hit. In CC&R controlled developments, there are maximum elevations for lots (determined by adding the elevation restriction to the pad level), meaning that beyond a certain point you'll be sacrificing pad level for interior height. Some communities limit their buildable elevation to 4 meters above pad level, which gives you in the mid-13-feet to build your house. Factor in the foot and a half or so for the roof tile and structure, and your highest ceiling can't be over 12 feet, gradually declining to 10 feet or so if there's a slope over that space. And because all roof areas can't be at the max elevation (or you lose "movement", which is the effect of a variation of roof height in different areas), you have obvious limitations.

And then there's the question of the surrounding lots. As previously discussed, oftentimes you're better off raising your lot elevation a meter if it means a difference of seeing ocean versus roof or laundry lines, leaving you with still less space. All of these considerations will come into play as the home's elevations are thought through, and while it isn't really up to you to define every element, it's helpful if you grasp the fundamentals at play.

When you get your cross-sections and your facades, first thing you should check is the maximum level of the main roof, to ensure that it doesn't exceed the allowed elevation. Don't assume the designer got it right – trust, but verify. And read your CC&Rs to establish whether you can have some design elements higher than the max elevation – most will allow things like chimneys, or domes, to exceed the envelope, but only by a certain amount, and only if they don't exceed a certain width. Understand what the exceptions are, so you can do a quick check to ensure compliance.

Roof Pitch and Drainage

You don't have to become an expert at roof design in order to check your roof. All plans will have a roof plan as part of the package, and what you want to look for is the amount of pitch on any sloped roofs. The reason you would need to care about this is because many CC&Rs mandate certain minimum roof pitches, and you want to catch any compliance issue before the HOA design review board does. The pitch degree will be a series of small numbers on the roof plan superimposed onto the roof drawing. If you can't find it, or don't understand what you're looking at, ask your designer.

You also want to ensure that the design has got drainage calculated from the roof. Again, you'd be surprised how many plans I've seen that don't have drainage thought through, or have the water egress landing onto the AC compressors or a garden area that would cause erosion. So what you want to verify is that your designer thought all this through, and that you aren't going to have a nightmare when the hurricanes deposit ten inches of water onto your roof in an hour.

Roof drainage should be depicted as a series of arrows indicating the gentle slope that will carry the water in the direction of the arrows. On flat roof areas, the pitch will be very, very gentle, almost imperceptible, but it needs to be there.

On terraces, you want to ensure that the elevations are a few cm lower for the terraces and decks. That will ensure that water won't pool on the deck, but rather will move to drainage points.

Some CC&Rs forbid flat roof areas, or more than a certain percentage of flat roof. Check yours to verify that what's drawn complies.

While you're looking at drainage, also check to ensure that any exterior planters have sensible drainage. I've seen them on finished homes where the ugly brown water from the planters dumps onto the entry cantera, with no drainage planned for that area, so the water just sits, stains, and acts as a mosquito breeding area. That shouldn't be you.

Again, the best rule of thumb is to look for the data, and if it isn't on the plan or you don't understand it, ask. It isn't rude, it's your plan, and you need to grasp all the info so you can be confident with what you're looking at.

Electric

The electric plan for your home is fairly easy to go through and understand. What you want to do is take each room, and look at the switches and outlets and such to ensure they seem logical to you.

As an example, when you first walk in your front door, there should be switches to turn on the lights of your living area, as well as to turn on the exterior lights. You might also want to have switches to turn on your ceiling fans in the living area, and also, depending upon the configuration of the home, also to light up at least a portion of the kitchen. You probably want those switches located where you can actually reach them when the door opens, rather than stuck behind the door. This seems like common sense, and it is, but you'd be surprised what can be left out of the mix. You also probably want switches to turn on the exterior lights in the same area, so when you leave you can easily access them.

If you have interior bathrooms that have no windows for ventilation, you'll want an exhaust fan. Check to ensure it's represented on the plan. If you want exhaust fans in all bathrooms, as some do, now's the time to pencil it in.

You also want to think through items like electrical outlets. You'll need sufficient outlets in the kitchen, for instance, to run all your appliances, as well as incidental appliances like blenders, toasters, countertop grills, etc. If you have an island, you'll probably want to ensure that there are outlets somewhere accessible on the island.

As far as wall outlets go, I usually put them about every eight to ten feet or so, unless they don't really make sense in that configuration. For example in a home office, you likely want more outlets, although the reality is that you'll be running all your important gear through a surge protector and battery backup. You also likely want to ensure there are phone lines there, as well as Internet, although most homes now run wireless for convenience as well as cost.

In bathrooms, each sink should get a couple of outlets, so all the miscellaneous gadgets we acquire can be plugged in without causing a traffic jam. You should also consider lights over mirrors, as if they aren't on the plan, they aren't going to be wired in.

As far as wiring for sound, my advice is get a specialist involved in the plan stage so that their input can make it to the blueprints. Sound is its own area of expertise, and with all the gizmos available these days, it's really best to defer to someone with the time and the ability to stay current. I tend to argue to keep it as simple as possible, as in Baja, complexity equates to maintenance headaches and chronic non-functionality.

When you're thinking electric, also think placement of overhead fans. You'll want overhead fans in most major areas, such as in each bedroom, and in the great-room. Just confirm that there are fans where you'll need them, and that the switches to turn them on and off are in logical places.

And confirm that you have adequate exterior lighting, as well as lighting in and around your pool area, including in the pool for the waterproof lights. Probably want to confirm a switch or two there or near there so as to be able to turn them on and off, as well as to operate the Jacuzzi, if you have one.

The last piece of the electrical plan is to verify where the breaker panel(s) is going to go. Make sure you're comfortable with the location, and know where it is.

Plumbing

Plumbing is one of those things you really don't need to spend a ton of time contemplating. Basically, you want water running to all faucets, and drains returning the flow. Toilets get their own system of return. Showers drain where the faucets do. Pretty straightforward.

It can get more complicated when you have water effects, but not that much more complicated. Water running to the effect, drains taking away.

The point to this guide isn't to train or encourage you to draft your own plans – rather, it's to arm you with enough info to be able to do reasonable checks on what you're handed by your designer. Plumbing doesn't require hours of consideration beyond the obvious.

There are, however, what I call the forgotten details. Hose bibs are one of those. Most homes require hose bibs in at least four or five spots, such as near the garage, on the decks for easy hose down, near planters and key gardening areas, etc. And yet many plans don't contain them – they're an afterthought to be dealt with once the plan is being built. You might want to get a jump on things and think about them in the plan stage – remember that this is the step by step description of your house, and if it isn't on the plan, it won't be bid.

Also, might want to check to make sure that any outdoor showers, such as for pool rinse off, are defined on the plan. Same for hot water heaters – you generally want several for larger homes, so that the hot water doesn't have too far to travel to get to a tap. I will often split them up on different sides of the house to ensure fairly close runs. Nobody likes waiting forever for hot water.

Finally, check for the location of the hydro pump system. This is the system that will pump water into and around the house, and supply pressure to all the faucets and showers. In the United States, we take for granted being hooked up to city water and power and sewage. In Mexico, it's more like a boat or an RV – each home requires its own pressure system to drive the water, its own treatment plant to process the waste water (unless you're one of the lucky few who are actually on city sewage), and its own storage tank (cistern) to hold bathing and drinking water.

For the latter reason, you'll want to ensure that the designer has specified a cistern, which is a water storage tank for the home that the city water replenishes. You'll be thankful you have that when city water is disrupted for weeks when a big hurricane hits – it's a mandatory item as far as I am concerned. Ten thousand liters is good, twenty is better for larger places.

I will usually put the hydro pump in the garage, or in an equipment area in or near the house, as the shorter the runs the more consistent the pressure. Cisterns I usually put under the garage floor, or any place where I need to occupy space instead of using dirt.

Pool equipment will need its own equipment area, so verify that your designer thought about where it will go. Proximity to the pool is key for this gear, as the longer the run, the harder the pump needs to work. And of course, also check to verify there's electricity going there. Seems obvious, but hey…

Confirm with your designer where the hot water heater(s) will go, and discuss the alternatives for hot water. Conventional propane boilers are the most trouble-free, however on larger homes you probably will want several, for various zones in the house. Most folks want hot water within thirty seconds or so of turning on a tap. Sometimes it can take a bit longer, depending on the length of the pipe run, however the home should be designed with delivery time in mind. "Instant on" heaters are also nice, however they have run length limitations, generally limited to twenty feet or so. Because they're also gas, they need to go outside for ventilation and safety reasons, creating a placement issue if you decide to populate the house with a bunch of them.

Forget about electric water heaters. They'll bankrupt you in Baja, where electricity is expensive. Solar water heaters are worth investigating, however they're pricey here, generally costing four times as much as conventional heaters. If the price comes down, that would be a great way to go with the technology.

Air Conditioning

Part of planning the house and going through the blueprints involves thinking through the type of air conditioning you'll be using, as the two different possible approaches involve significantly different aesthetic and planning issues.

There are two types of AC in Baja – Mini-Split systems, and Fan & Coil.

Mini-splits are the plastic appliances that hang on the wall by the ceiling. They were originally designed as retro-fit solutions for homes that didn't want window or wall AC units – the old fashioned boxes on the outside of the house. Mini-splits are manufactured by any number of companies, and can be found in most retail and office environments, as well as lower-end to mid-level homes. The thermostat is located inside the actual unit – it's self contained, and comes with a remote for operation.

Fan & Coil is the type of AC you find in most higher-end hotels, where there's a grid on the wall through which cool air flows, controlled by a thermostat on the wall. This is a much more elegant way to handle AC, as it's unobtrusive, and can be incorporated into the overall flow of the home with no disruptions.

It kills me when I walk into multi-million dollar homes, and see unsightly plastic boxes on the walls instead of grids. The clients maybe saved ten grand on the total build cost, and they now have an eyesore for life, as well as an AC solution most view as low-end.

Both Fan & Coil and Mini-split systems are zoned, room by room, so you can cool only the areas you're in. The only major difference is the aesthetic, as well as a cost difference – Fan & Coil is more expensive due to all the ducting required, as well as the sheetrock to hide the units.

There's no such thing as central air here, as you would go broke cooling the entire house every time you wanted AC. There's only zoned AC, and of those, I will only install Fan & Coil in my builds. Going with Mini-Splits is just a lousy way to save money – if it's that big a deal, I'd rather squeeze somewhere else than put eyesores where everyone can see them.

I've seen some put Mini-Splits in housings or boxes to disguise the appliance, however that backfires due to the design of the units. They're designed to have free airflow, and when that's restricted, even a little, by a housing or a grid assembly in front of them, the life expectancy of the units drops considerably as the units have to work harder. You won't notice it in the first couple years, but you'll be burning the units out way earlier than you should as you own the home, and the replacement of the dead units will likely wind up costing you as much as if you had just gone with Fan & Coil in the first place.

Facades

Probably the most fun part about seeing your plans is viewing the facades – the drawings of what the exterior of the house will look like. Sure, floor plans give you a sense of the layout and the spaces, but actually seeing what looks like a real house is a thrill. Or at least it should be.

Different designers have different capabilities when it comes to drawing exteriors. Some do very primitive CAD drawings that look almost like line drawings, others do fully articulated exteriors that look like etchings, still others do highly detailed drawings that are almost photographic in detail.

Whichever sort of exterior drawings you get, there are things to look for.

First, does the home look the way you thought it would? Does it resemble the photos you brought in? Is it the same style? Hopefully, it does, although I've often seen finished drawings that look, well, unfinished, to say the least. I think what happens is that clients don't really know what their finished drawings should look like, thus are just happy that they have some facades.

My perspective is that the more detailed and precise the exterior, the less ambiguity in terms of what the house will look like, thus the better for everyone.

When you get your facades, pay attention to the major items. Do the windows look the way you want them to? The doors? What about the treatment around the windows? How about the stonework? Columns? Trim? Is there adequate variation in the roof elevations, enough "movement?"

If you don't like something, now's the time to change it.

Additionally, you should get all the finishes called out on the plan. For example, the window sills should say, "Cantera" if you intend to use cantera. Ditto for the trim around the windows, and around the doors (if there is any). The material the window frames are made out of should be called out – if wood-look aluminum, the plan should specify that.

You want to eliminate a lack of specificity, and you want to understand what's being specified. This is the manual that will define how your house is finished, so pay attention to detail. You don't have to get everything defined here, but it's nice if you have most large items covered.

One item I strongly suggest you have articulated on the plan or on your finish list is the type of windows you want – as in, do you want windows that open sliding side to side, or do you want windows that open out, and if so, with a crank, or with a lever push? I tend to advise clients to go with windows that move side to side, as the wind can play hell with the sort that open out – a good blow hits one of those when it's open, and the window acts as a sail, damaging the mechanism, and possibly the glass and/or the frame. Many prefer the open out sort, however not once they've had to pay to replace crank mechanisms or damaged frames.

As you look at the drawings of the house, check to confirm that the facades tie into the floor plan and drainage and roof plans. If there's a roof drain articulated on the plan at the front right corner of the house, confirm the facade shows it. Again, you don't want differences between the various plans – they should tie together as different "views" of the same house.

Some folks will pay extra and get 3D renderings of their home, the better to visualize exactly what it will look like. This can be valuable, but isn't mandatory. I like 3D exteriors, however, as the more manifest the idea can be articulated on paper, the better your ability to make changes before the plan gets converted into steel and mortar.

Landscaping

Most CC&Rs will require a landscaping plan, which can be elaborately executed, or fairly simple – almost a placeholder.

I tend to favor the simple approach, as inevitably what's done to the finished home will be considerably different than what was conceived of by the home designer. Generally, a landscaping company will come in at the end of construction, and propose their vision of how to landscape the grounds. Alternatively, the clients will have had a year or so to develop more evolved ideas about how they want to treat the various areas.

In a perfect world, you would hire a landscape designer to spend a month on your plan before it gets stamped. In the real world, less than five percent of clients do this, for the aforementioned reasons.

How you handle it really is a matter of how much flexibility you want on the back end of the build. Most want as much as possible.

Before we get to the final sections covering other parts of your plan you need to consider, it's best at this point to discuss the actual material you'll be using to build the house. Reason it comes in at this stage is that once your plan is done, you'll need to get a structural plan created, and that structural plan will vary depending upon what material the home is built out of.

Materials

Probably the most critical piece of the process of specifying all the elements in your home is deciding what it will actually be made out of. To that end, this section will discuss the primary materials in use in Baja, and offer some observations as to their sundry positives and negatives. We'll start with cement, and move to synthetics.

Concrete continues to escalate in price, as steel has done as long as I can remember, which is now creating an interesting situation when it comes to alternative materials. Couple of years ago, I pretty much did everything in concrete block, as the various foam panel products were just too expensive for my clients.

Back then, you could figure that the total cost of a build would increase by ten percent or so if you went with panel. Maybe more, at the end of the day. And while there's no dispute that panel or many of the synthetic alternatives is vastly superior to concrete from a thermal perspective, the cost factor wasn't greeted with a ton of enthusiasm by my build clients.

My stopgap solution was to insulate the walls that would get the most sun, usually with some sort of high-density foam. While not perfect, it was way cheaper than the panel alternative, and the thermal transfer to the air from the hot block was largely reduced to the point where it was a non-issue.

But now concrete has increased so much, along with runaway steel prices, I've increasingly been using alternative materials, although panel still remains cost prohibitive vis a vis other synthetic possibilities.

And there are many alternatives, although most still just think of panel. Not the case anymore. There are other materials one can incorporate that will achieve remarkable thermal benefits without skyrocketing the price, so I use those instead. After all, when the cost delta is minimal on the finished product, why not get the thermally superior solution? I've been doing hybrid techniques, building some walls out of foam with a concrete core, and some out of autoclave aerated concrete. I still use regular concrete for many applications, as it's predictable and well-understood by the crews here, however I'm moving to alternatives in order to get a better end product at the same cost.

The result is a thermally efficient home that will stay cooler in the heat, and consume far less energy. At a few percentage points above the same overall project price as concrete and block.

Concrete basically stinks as a temperature barrier. You couldn't really do worse, whereas products like autoclave aerated concrete, or panel, or other foam-based solutions, have limited thermal transfer – meaning that the outside of the wall could be a hundred and forty degrees, but the inside of the wall would be cool to the touch. I don't really defend concrete, as experience quickly shows that it's boiling hot to the touch on sun-receiving walls, whereas any of the synthetic alternatives are cool. Self-explanatory. Don't believe me? Just go to one of my builds, touch a concrete area, and then touch a synthetic area. Night and day.

As with most things, there are tradeoffs, and the raw material still winds up costing more, however there are very real savings on some of the detail work on things like arched windows and doors, where the synthetic products are much faster to work with. It's always a case of balancing the benefits against the price, and trying to find the right combination for the particular client. As concrete continues to get pricier, the alternatives start looking much more reasonable.

More to follow in the next sections dealing with materials in more depth. For now, let's just focus on the idea that you can make choices that will result in a cooler home, for not that much more money.

If you can have a significantly cooler home for, say, one percent to two percent of the total home cost as a premium, wouldn't you at least take a much harder look at it? I would. And that's the net effect of what's been happening, although panel is still moving price-wise in a manner that has it costing around ten percent more than concrete. That's one of the reasons I personally favor other synthetics, and a hybrid concrete and synthetic approach, over a pure panel approach – the cost just can't be justified for my clients versus other equally effective materials.

Overall, it's good for everyone to build out of thermally efficient products, as energy consumption is radically reduced, as are system requirements. What do I mean? Well, a home I'm building now, using hybrid construction techniques and materials, will require maybe thirty to forty percent less AC installed than an all concrete block house with no insulation. That means just the opening salvo of raw cost to build the place is lower from an AC equipment perspective. All good, as that savings can further go to offset the premium it costs to build out of synthetics. And on an operating basis, it will translate into less energy consumed, as it takes far less time to cool a room if there's minimal thermal inefficiency. Over the years, that will make for a big savings over your neighbor whose home is built out of block, assuming the same cooling habits.

You're still going to always have some inefficiency, due to niggling items like windows. There are more efficient windows out there, too, however they cost significantly more than regular glass, and we are then back to the cost/benefit argument. As with all things, it's not a perfect world, but the goal should always be to achieve the coolest house you can without breaking the bank. If one thinks in terms of total project cost versus material cost, it can make a lot of sense to move in the direction of the synthetics.

While we're discussing heat issues and energy consumption, I highly recommend looking at the new generations of LED bulbs, as incandescent lights generate considerable heat and are hugely inefficient, whereas alternatives like fluorescent don't (and consume far less power than incandescent). But LED's consume a fraction of what fluorescents do, making them interesting long term solutions. As a cost comparison, a regular bulb might cost a buck and generate 60 watts of light. A fluorescent that generates the same amount of light might be $4 and draw 13 watts. And an LED might cost $120 for an amber natural light type bulb that generates 60 watts of light, but will draw less than 1 watt. If you're in a solar state of mind, that translates into 60 bulbs in the house drawing as much as a single 60 watt incandescent bulb – and they last pretty much forever. Which means less solar equipment required for lighting, which translates into cost savings on the front end which can largely offset the cost of the bulbs. Savings for on-the-grid homes would be equivalent over the longer haul in terms of lower energy bills. Just a thought, since we are talking energy efficiency.

This section's conclusions will change if the cost to build out of panel is at or below the cost to build out of concrete block. We aren't there yet, but the good news is that every day brings us closer to where some of the synthetic alternatives are more in line with traditional construction techniques and materials, creating a win/win situation for everybody.

I also support using synthetics in areas where they cuts costs without impacting quality. For instance, in trim around rooflines, there are moldings with concrete-like exteriors that are indistinguishable from stone, and install in a matter of days. Nobody can tell the difference from two feet away, and they last forever. I use acres of foam in floors and roofs, for the insulation and sound deadening reasons. I also like synthetic wood for exposed beams on ceilings. You can't tell a difference, and there's hardly any weight. Everyone wins on that one, especially the trees.

Let's talk counters and tile. Counters made from Corian and other synthetics? Leave it for the tract home in the States. Use granite and marble here. There's no comparison, so don't bother with the synthetics. And ceramic tile is fine for low-end homes, but you don't want it anywhere near higher-quality homes. It's penny-wise but pound foolish, and looks cheap. Don't play Scrooge on your flooring and counters. As an example, travertine isn't much more expensive than synthetics, and is way nicer. So don't be a cheapskate. Pony up for stone. That's just not where you want to save money.

Now that we've discussed the cost and thermal characteristics, let's look at the most accepted building materials and consider their merits and drawbacks.

First is concrete, and its partner steel. These are the most economical materials to build out of in Baja, and most homes you see are built using them. If you want to keep your costs lowest, specify that you want your home built out of concrete block. This is achieved in the bid via the *memorio de calculo*.

Concrete and Steel

Concrete block is ubiquitous in Baja construction. It's by far the most common material, even in most high–end homes. I use a lot of it, and while it isn't good from a thermal perspective when compared to synthetics, it's stable, understood, and strong. Still, there are things one needs to be aware of when considering concrete.

Don't fall for using inferior block quality like 10 centimeter block, versus standard 15 centimeter, for exterior walls. Don't do it. As an aside, I spec in 20 centimeter block from only two suppliers for my exterior walls when they aren't going to be built out of a synthetic, as well as for all retaining walls. I will occasionally use 15 centimeter or even 10 centimeter in areas where I want to maximize interior space, but won't do it for most as it's not a great tradeoff. In a hall, or a closet or bath, where 2 inches more on each side could make a difference, I'll take a hard look at it, but mostly I will stick with 20 cm for exterior walls, and 15 for interior. While there's nothing wrong with using 15 for an entire home, and I've done it for budget reasons when the client is trying to squeeze costs, I really prefer 20 for exterior walls due to the look and the finish. The only caveat to this is if I am using 15 centimeter autoclave aerated concrete, I will match that with 15 centimeter block for uniform wall thickness.

Now I'll volunteer a secret from the bowls of building arcania. All concrete block isn't the same. There are radically different qualities of block, from pathetic to pristine. Why should you care? Because houses built out of junk don't wear well, and tend to crack apart, and have all sorts of problems over time – and if you're a corner cutter as a builder with your block, you probably are cutting other important corners. Obviously, you want the best stuff you can get your house built out of, however that often isn't an imperative shared by your builder. I can't tell you how many sites I've seen where the block is miserable quality, virtually guaranteeing a crack-fest in the finished home down the road, and at worst, a dangerous structure.

What do I mean? Let me share a true story. I was doing my usual Sunday inspection of some of my projects (I like to go out when there are no crews, and check out the quality of the build at my own pace, uninterrupted by noise and bustle), and noted a new build going up near one of my sites. I always like to see what the competition is doing, so I went over to see what the plan looked like, and suss the materials they were using. The news wasn't good (or rather, it was great for me, as there was no comparison).

First, the block was garbage. Both the 6 inch (15 centimeter) and 8 inch (20 centimeter) block sitting at the site was miserable stuff, with the larger block used for the retaining walls. The block quality was obvious from a dozen yards away. Uneven edges, a crumbly look, porous surfaces – junky block. Now, you'll likely never see the actual block used for your house, but let me pass on a tip – cheap quotes usually equate to cheap materials, which in turn produce lousy quality finished product.

I would have rejected the block on that site out of hand, and yet it was being used to build a home in a marquis community. To test my visual observation, I did simple field drop testing. To do this, you pick up a random block, hold it at chest height, and drop it onto dirt (not pavement). If it breaks apart, you have junk. If it holds together, it's good block. Very straightforward. So I picked up a 6 inch block, held it out, and let go. Poof. It shattered into about a dozen pieces. Picked up another one, did the same, and same result. Not good. Then I did the same with the 8 inch they were using for the retaining walls, where the block is part of the structural integrity of the wall. Poof. Crumblier than coffee cake. And this was what was going to ensure the house stayed put in a seismic event or a hurricane.

I then went over to my site, and did the same thing with my block. Thunk. Solid, no break. Another one, thunk, same thing. The security guard at another builder's site across the way laughed, and gave the thumb's up. He'd watched the whole thing, and was also shaking his head over the block on the other site. This was one of the lowest end guys on that crew, assigned to security work overnight, and even he knew the difference.

The point is, you really have to be careful of what your builder is using. I only get block from two companies, whose quality has been uniform over multiple sites and years. I even send my concrete and block out periodically to an independent lab, just to verify that our vendors are behaving. One of the easiest ways to ensure that your builder is using decent block is to insist upon spot inspections of each load that shows up. After the first couple once the walls are up, you're out of the woods on that issue.

Another thing to add to your caution list is steel. You have no idea whether your builder is using certified steel with the requisite tensile strength, or black market steel, which is generally way weaker (and cheaper, of course). Rebar all sort of looks the same, but it isn't. There are a number of qualified providers here in Baja, and they're widely known as dealing exclusively in certified steel. Ask your builder who they're getting their steel from – what provider. If you have any niggling doubts, ask to see *facturas* from the provider.

I try to explain these things to prospective clients, but some don't want to believe it – they just want to believe that if they're super-duper hard negotiators, they can get the killer deal on their build....you know, just because. They don't want to believe they could be getting taken on things they never considered or realized existed. You don't want to fall into that trap – understand that there are a million ways to skimp or cheat if your builder is so motivated, and you'll never catch most of them. But you can at least take a hard look at the obvious items like block and steel, and confirm that it's good quality.

As discussed, while I prefer hybrid technique where I use some synthetic material for exterior walls and concrete for interior, many homes are built entirely out of block, and there's nothing wrong with the approach except for the thermal drawbacks. When cost is an issue, block is the way to go. You need to have decided that question before your home goes out for bid, though, as the decision is an important cost one.

Synthetics

The most common synthetic in use in Baja is 3-D panel, which is a Styrofoam panel with a metal wire grid exterior for structural strength. A hardened concrete material is coated onto either side of the panel's grid, and the end result is as hard as concrete block. It requires different structural considerations and is theoretically faster to put up than block, and has radically superior thermal properties. The positives are the faster construction time (if that's actually achieved in the real world by the crew working on the house) and superior thermal characteristics. The negative is cost. At the time of this edition's release, the overall cost difference between block and panel is roughly ten percent. To put that into perspective, a $900,000 build in block will be a roughly $1 million build in panel. While it's true that you'll save a bunch on AC over the years, the question is really whether you'll save $100,000 worth, or for my clients, the question is how long it would take for the panel to pay itself off.

It turns out that's a fairly simple equation. You won't have to spend as much on AC equipment. So let's say you save $10,000 there. Super. Now you need to calculate how much you'll save in AC usage due to the superior thermal characteristics.

If your average power bill is $6,000 per year, with panel it might drop to $3,000. So your savings might be $3,000 per year, plus the $10,000 you saved on the front end. You can see how it could take a long time, as in longer than anyone reading this book will likely live, to see a payback. But it's actually worse when you take into account time value of money.

If you took that same $90,000 or so and put it into a three and a half percent interest bearing account, it would generate about $3,000 per year – basically the cost of the AC usage you would have saved. The difference is that at the end of, oh, thirty years, you still have the $90,000, whereas in the panel scenario it's gone and you're at breakeven with nothing to show for it. If you can do better than three and a half percent with your investments, you're net ahead substantially.

I've tried to make the numbers work, but they don't. Which is why economically speaking, panel doesn't work for my clients at this time. There are many builders who convince their clients that the math does vet, and good on them, but I can't for the life of me make it work. Thus, panel isn't in my mix as long as the cost delta is ten percent. Additionally, panel can look blotchy or wavy once it's finished – more often than not, the mortar on the exterior looks amateurish, which is why many panel homes are sponge painted on the exterior to hide the blotchiness. Even builders who have been using it for years have the same issue, so it's just another one of the distinctive and unique limitations that all materials have.

There are other synthetic solutions, however, that I do favor, albeit in conjunction with concrete. One of these is foam with cavities into which you pour concrete and place rebar, achieving a thermal barrier with concrete characteristics. It's not practical to build an entire house out of the material, however I've used it on walls, and it works well in the target areas. I've also seen some builders doing most of a home out of it, so you could probably make a case for it. It's cheaper than panel, but at the end of the day, still more expensive than block, far as I can tell.

Another is one that most of postwar Germany is built out of – autoclave aerated concrete. I use this extensively now for exterior walls that will receive sun. It too is more expensive than block, however I've experienced genuine savings in terms of labor (it goes up quickly) and cutting in electric and plumbing, so at the end of the day the real cost isn't much more than block, which is why I use it. It has a very high thermal inertia, which translates into keeping cool rooms cool while the sun beats down on the wall's exterior.

The message in all this is that the cost to bid as reflected in a bid is a function of what materials one decides to use to build the house. Save some on AC equipment by using hybrid technique, pay more for some synthetic materials, but if it nets out as a one percent or so overall difference than using block, you're a winner, as the house will be way more pleasant to live in, and you really will see some savings on energy consumption to keep it cool. Talk to your designer about what to use, and make it part of the bid, again, eliminating ambiguity down the road.

Hi-Tech or KISS

You're getting ready to build, and the question comes up, "Hey, what about all that high tech stuff we're bombarded with as "must have" up in the States?"

Opinions vary greatly on this topic, largely based on whether the person you ask makes money from your deciding to be as technology-driven as possible. There are a few pretty skilled companies in town who can wire up your home to be a smart house, with every imaginable contraption present, making your life "simpler." Whether you decide to go this route is immaterial to your builder, beyond his ensuring that the home has wire runs going wherever you want.

I tend to lean towards the KISS (Keep It Simple, Stupid) approach in deciding these things.

You moved to Baja to do what? Complicate your life, or simplify it? Accumulate more gadgetry, or less? Philosophically, we're fed a diet of consumption and acquisitiveness in every area of our life when we're *Norteamericanos*. So is it desirable to import that South of the border? You can, but should you?

There's my Luddite take on it. Now to the more practical aspects of the question.

Anyone who's been through one of our hurricanes is familiar with the power surges and brownouts, and complete blackouts, that characterize those deluges. And don't forget, up until recently, blackouts were fairly regular occurrences. I have a clock radio that runs twenty minutes fast every month, even though it's digital. I've had three phones burn out, inexplicably. My computers have problems. I had a fax machine fry. Even though I have surge protectors all over the place, and battery backups, Cabo's desire to fry my gear seems to win every time.

Now consider a smart house. Computer controlled, your blinds go up and down, your AC is automated, lights come on and off, data streams all over the house...Yeah. Right. Why not just hop into your teleporter and dematerialize to Australia while you're at it? Reality is that Baja has advanced markedly in just the last few years, but NY it isn't. The infrastructure is playing catch-up, and to incorporate complex technology into your life isn't all that great an idea. At least not yet. My advice is wire the house up so that it's smart house "ready" if you really want that technology, but hold off on buying the boxes. I have friends in the States who have three separate systems, and the highest paid geeks constantly working on their home, and they still can't get things to work as advertised. Call me a cynic, but I lean towards simpler systems and approaches.

You can always add it later. If you think you need it. Which you probably won't once you've been living here for a few months.

When you're considering what to wire, I'd say Ethernet, phone, and anything else you like, just so the cable is there if you decide to install something later. And now there's cheap technology enabling data transmission over copper wire, so even the Ethernet probably isn't necessary.

I do recommend alarm systems, for peace of mind, so it's a good idea to wire for that, although many alarms are now wireless. I also like security cams for areas where I can't easily see, to make sure the dogs and kids and whatnot are OK.

What about solar power, and generators?

There are solar power solutions that can run much of your house some of the time at a reasonably economic level. The technology gets more affordable every year, so that's something to watch as power bills continue to escalate, although you need to check with your CC&Rs to see whether you're allowed to have solar panels in your community. Also, you'll need someplace fairly large to store the batteries and the inverter for the solar. At the time of the publishing of this first edition, you should be able to get enough system to run your 4500 sq. foot house, except for the pool and the AC, for around $45,000 or so, plus or minus twenty percent depending upon how many appliances and pumps and fans and lights you have. Given that an average power bill here is anywhere from $6,000 and up per year, if you can eliminate ninety percent of that, you can see where your payback hits at around eight years. As solar prices drop over the next thousand days, maybe you can get payback to around five years, at which point I tend to say it's a no–brainer, assuming you live here year-round.

If you have the cash, I say, "Why not?" You'll be the envy of everyone you know the next time a storm knocks out the power for a few days (or weeks). Same thing for generators, although I say invest in a propane or diesel generator versus a gasoline-powered unit. Gasoline generators are little bombs waiting to go off at the worst possible moment, usually when the roads are flooded and the hospitals are closed. I wouldn't recommend a gas generator to my worst enemy. A propane generator hooked into your propane line is a different story, as you don't have to contend with the joy of pouring highly flammable and explosive liquid into the device when it's smoking hot. Diesel generators present their own issues, and unless you intend to run that baby almost all the time, I'd shy away, as they're more expensive, you'll have fuel issues (diesel will get algae in it unless you have a filtration system for the fuel tank – and you can't really use the fuel for anything else but the generator, unlike propane which will run your stove, dryer, hot water heater, etc.).

So the short version is, absolutely get a generator (propane-fueled) and absolutely get solar power (if you can afford it and the rules allow it). Being self-contained is always a good idea in Baja.

Structural Plan and Memorio De Calculo, Other Plans

Once your plan has made it through the entire process, and has been approved by the homeowner's association architectural design review board (assuming there is one), and you've decided what material you'll build it out of, it's time to get a structural plan done, including a *memorio de calculo.*

An observation about HOA review boards. They look at things like whether the home is within the elevation allowances, whether it sits within the buildable envelope of the lot plan, and whether it conforms to the various and sundry requirements of the CC&Rs. They don't check to confirm that the plans are well done, or that the home can actually be built, or that the spaces are adequate, or that it's a good or even an advisable plan. They don't look at the interior at all, and it isn't their concern what goes on inside, or whether it's structurally sound or a good plan from a design standpoint. There's nobody to do that, but you, which is why you need to spend some time with your plan and get familiar with it. You are the safety net. Your designer may be great, or horrible, but at the end of the day it's your house, thus you, for better or for worse, need to take some responsibility for acting as the gatekeeper on the plan.

That said, someone has to figure out how to keep it from falling down. That's a registered, licensed engineer. What he will do is take the plans, and then create a structural plan, which will articulate precisely how many beams, with what PSI (or Kg per cm) concrete and what gauge rebar, will be required to build the house safely. This plan will look like a skeleton of the home seen from the top, as it will show the placement of each column and beam. It's highly detailed, as the columns and beams are what support the house – they're the backbone. Regardless of what material is to be used – foam panel, concrete block, autoclave aerated concrete, hybrid materials – you'll require a structural plan for the building department to issue a permit.

Creation of this plan generally is a two week to one month job.

Once it's created, the engineer and architect will also generate a, *"Memorio de Calculo".* This is basically, for lack of a better description, a recipe for the home, with a detailed list of ingredients. It will define how many pieces of rebar, how many beams, how many gas lines, etc. You need a *memorio de calculo* to get any sort of intelligent or meaningful bid. It's impossible to cost a home's construction without knowing all the elements that will need to be included, which is why I always crack up when I hear statements like, "I talked to a guy who can build my house for $50 per foot less than anyone else can!" We will discuss why this is hogwash in the next chapter, but one clue is that absent a *memorio de calculo* and about two weeks of work costing every element in the home, there's no way to know how much anything will cost, even as a ballpark. The *memorio* defines that, as does a list of finishes, which should be part of it, or a separate single page sheet.

That will articulate the detail on the finishes, such as, "Floor, travertine marble, 16X16 inch, crème, special select grade" or "Window Sill, Cantera", or "Carpentry – doors, mahogany with stain to be chosen by client, and Cabinets, knotty alder faces" or "Yeso (plaster), smooth finish, 2.5 cm thick, rounded corners" or "Fan Coil AC, 20 Tons, Trane or similar brand". That list, again, eliminates ambiguity, and allows you to understand exactly what you're getting. You want to confirm that the broad stroke items are all listed – flooring, wall treatments, counter material, window types, door types, cabinetry type, roof material, pool material, deck material, window trim, and any flourishes like cantera fountains or gargoyles or the like.

Finally, you should get several other plans before you start building, although different designers will treat these as optional versus included. Carpentry plans are a good idea, as they enable you to define precisely what your cabinets and closets will look like. Some wait and do these with the builder at an additional cost, working with the carpenter they'll use, others prefer to get it all defined on the front end. I prefer the front end. A flooring plan is also a good idea, as it spells out precisely what patterns will be laid in your house. And an AC plan is a positive, as it will define ceiling treatments and levels. All these can be handled post hoc, however if you have the time, I'd shoot for getting it all defined up front. Having said that, any or all of these can, and often are, completed by around month number four of construction.

To get meaningful bids, which is what the next chapter will focus on, you need to ensure that you're getting apples to apples quotations using all the same assumptions. The *memorio de calculo* and the list of finishes, combined with the plan, will get you much closer to that goal. Check the list, and confirm that everything is what you want. If you want granite counters, and they're listed as tile, now's the time to change it. Ditto for the rest, although a good builder will make suggestions along the way to save you money or improve the design. Which brings me to the next section of this chapter, and one you should take to heart.

Change Orders

Why are change orders being briefly covered in the Blueprint chapter?

Because the quantity of change orders will usually be based upon how much time and attention you put into your blueprint.

Change orders reflect a change or addition to the plan. Obviously, that means that something either wasn't articulated the way you wanted it, or it wasn't on the plan at all. In either case, change orders will generally cost you more money, and delay your build. The reason is simple. Any change reflects something other than what was bid, which is what's in the plan and articulated in your build agreement and your finish list and *memorio de calculo*. Thus, it wasn't costed. Thus, it's an addition. And it wasn't factored into the schedule.

So the final thought you should have as you leave this section covering your plans is that blueprints are the recipe and schematic for your build, and the less precise they are, the more changes you'll be making as you go along. Which is a strong argument for taking the extra time to master the various areas I've described, using the software I advise downloading, and thinking through items that are really important to you. You can always change your mind later, but it usually costs more to do so.

Summary

You've gone through your blueprints, thought through the important elements, and verified that the plan contains all the items you wanted. After weighing the merits of various materials, you've decided what approach you want to take, and are now ready to go find a builder. The following chapter will cover how to select a builder without choosing a wrong number, and how to structure a deal that will achieve your goals.

Checklist

- Contract Review, Software Download
- Time with Designer
- Score the Floorplan
- Confirm Elevations
- Review Roof and Drainage

- Review Electric

- Review Plumbing/Hydraulic

- Review Facades

- Review Landscaping

- Consider Material Choices

- Get Structural/*Memorio De Calculo*

CHAPTER 4 - BIDS AND CONTRACTS

Overview

In this chapter we'll go through how to qualify builder candidates, we'll review the bid process, and finally go over what a construction contract should contain. We'll also try to dispel unrealistic beliefs about what is and isn't possible in Baja in terms of cost, as well as arm you with enough info about how to evaluate builders to be dangerous by the end of this section.

Perhaps the best way to start off is to review some horror stories arising from some assumptions we Gringos tend to have about Baja in general.

One of the most difficult things for newcomers to understand is that it's far more expensive to build here than imagined. The reasons are manifest. They include the fact that very little is produced locally – everything has to get here via truck, down 900 miles of peninsula, or via air or ocean. Consider the price of gas in Mexico, and you'll quickly see how that creates a rather marked premium for most everything. Wood, steel, most industrial products, all finish materials, all appliances...essentially everything's brought in, either from mainland Mexico, or imported.

Also, most everything's denominated in dollars, due to wild currency fluctuations, as well as the import/export market. Anything bought in the United States is denominated in greenbacks, and most items that are shipped abroad are also denominated in dollars, as the lion's share of the production is for export and the producers are used to pricing in dollars.

Add to that the fact that the building technique and materials are different. In Baja, we build as in the United States before World War II. Back then, buildings were made out of concrete and rebar. What happened is that when all the GIs returned home, builders scrambled to satisfy the massive instant demand for housing by turning to "temporary" construction techniques and materials – slapping up some two by fours, nailing sheetrock with some insulation to them, and squirting stucco on the outside. Everyone was amazed that people bought the resultant structures, in droves, and the builders never looked back. Why take a year or two building a home when you could slap one together in a matter of a few months? Sure, they burned easily, and were noisy and shoddily built, but hey, it cost a lot less to build them, and people seemed satisfied....

That became the norm for residential construction, especially in the West. If you go to older sections of LA or Long Beach you'll find all the pre-war homes are built out of concrete, and are still standing. They don't rot, don't burn, don't mold, and don't degrade over time. Every fifty years or so you have to chip out the old copper pipes and replace them, but other than that, they'll be there two hundred years from now. Same for the places here, with the exception that we don't use copper for the pipes anymore.

And finally, for all the apparent activity, we aren't on the mainland, and there really isn't that much building going on compared to that area. So the talent pool is relatively small, and the labor is paid more. It costs way more to live here than on mainland. It's about as expensive as San Diego. That means that many are making the kind of money that their skill brings in San Diego, just to survive here. Sure, you can find guys who will work for fractions, but they're at the bottom of the skill ladder, and new arrivals. Not many will work for less than sustenance – they'll just go home if they're going to make little or nothing.

I tell folks that the correct way to think about this area is like it's Hawaii. Just as building there costs far more than on the mainland, so it is here. We're both separated by a body of water, and the desolate two lane road from TJ isn't much of a commerce superhighway.

So there's no free lunch, and the days of being able to build for a fraction of what you could in the United States are history. Sure, if you want a simple, barrio-level construction with extremely rough finishes and lackadaisical workmanship, you can do that for bargain pricing, but it will look it. It won't look like the more quality-driven homes that have appeared here over the last five years. You still see that lower level being built far out in the East Cape and up toward Todo Santos and Pescadero, and in La Paz, but in Cabo, it's dead money, as few buyers want that sort of product any more.

The big question is always, "What will it cost to build my house?" The answer is, depends on who builds it, and what quality level it's built to, and what finishes are used.

By now, you probably have a fair idea of what it costs to build the house you designed, as you've spoken with others in your target community, and done your homework on what the quality level you are after generally costs. There will always be a range, and the range is typically defined on a spectrum from the highest-priced, most established builders, where there's essentially no risk in terms of execution and they've done it dozens of times before, to new entrants in the market who are trying to win market share by price.

Understanding this, let's move forward and cover the nuts and bolts of the builder selection and qualification process, the details of the bid process, and finish up by examining the contract phase, listing mandatory protections and discussing various payment schemes. The goal of the chapter is to have you completely confidant in the builder selection process by the time you've finished it, and ensure that you have adequate protections so that you can't be taken to the cleaners.

How Do I Know Who To Trust To Build My House?

This is the sixty-four thousand dollar question that runs through everyone's mind as they move forward towards building their dream house. It's a good question, given the myriad horror stories that are the legacy of the area.

There are any number of ways to get builder candidates, and to qualify who's competent. The most typical is to drive around your community, and see who's building there already. That's not a bad way of doing it, as you can at least see finished product and get a feel for what the quality of the work looks like. Another way is to ask around and find out who built places you like. Yet another way is to ask your broker, however that runs the risk that they're getting a financial incentive for steering the builder your way. My advice is to look at established players with a decent book of business and a library of already-built homes, who builds the quality level you're considering in communities you like – preferably yours.

The designer you worked with is always a good bet, assuming they fit the last criteria as a builder. If you don't like the work they've done as a builder, however, you're best off looking to professionals who build homes, as opposed to designers who don't build to your quality spec.

You want a builder who is currently building at least a few homes at your target quality level, and who's busy enough that they're financially stable, but not so busy that you're going to be one of half dozen or more homes they do in a year. The reason you want to avoid the larger producers is that building in Mexico is very much tied to the quality of the direct supervision, and it's hard to keep quality at a high level when you take on too much work. I've found that I can reasonably do three to four homes a year to the quality level I want to build at. I could do more, but I'd have to delegate more than I want to and I'd be afraid of seeing quality slip. Some builders here can do five or six competently if they have two decades of infrastructure established, however you'll wind up paying a premium for them as all that infrastructure costs to keep in place.

Big names around town can easily get all the way up to $500 per square foot and beyond – but they generally build 10,000 foot homes and up, and they're world famous. If you're interested in one of the Rolls Royce builders, they're easy to find, as they're literally household names, and are in all the books.

Most clients don't fall into that caviar lifestyle profile. Most want a qualified, good quality builder who will perform to their desired quality level, and will do so at a relatively reasonable cost. They want someone who'll deliver in a reasonable timeframe, and without unpleasant surprises. Seems fair.

One problem is that as you go downstream from the top-tier big names, the quality and the reliability start going all over the map. What I think of as the crème of the well established middle-tier guys – MCA, Gravi, AIA, Malberg, etc. – all do excellent work. As you move down the price spectrum from there, however, results tend to become less predictable. Some do excellent and dependable work, some routinely take 18 months to build a 1 year house, with thirty percent cost over-runs and iffy quality, and some build regrettable homes that nobody is happy about. Toward the bottom of the range are operators who are flat out larcenous, or incompetent, or both. Again, not all, or even most, but more than a few. This has nothing to do with Mexican versus Gringo operators, either, as there are plenty of Gringos doing less than stellar work. This just has to do, mainly, with two constants – it's hard to build good quality work in Baja due to a vast array of cultural, environmental, and skill-set reasons; and, there will always be those who prefer to take shortcuts or to take advantage of the client, versus doing the work.

Often, a giveaway on this is when a bid is out of the range – everyone comes in within $20 a foot of each other, and one is $40 or $50 lower. You need to ask yourself what secret sauce that lowball bid contains. My experience has been that it's generally one of two things: The builder can't build the home for what he's quoting in order to get you on the line, and intends to change things once you're pregnant and can't change horses, or he intends to take dangerous and reckless shortcuts at every turn – shoddy workmanship, junk materials, poor quality everything.

I suggest that when you select builder candidates, that you use the same qualifying mechanisms as you did selecting a designer:

1) Look at some of their actual, recent work at the price point you're considering building. You don't want to see what they can do at double the per square foot costs that fit your budget, you want to see what they can do at the price and quality level you're talking. I mention this because it's not uncommon for some builders to show $350 per foot homes they built for themselves or for spec, and to represent that as typical of their work. It won't be. Building for yourself where budget isn't a primary concern is far easier than building for clients on a budget. You want to see actual homes built for actual clients, in or around the pricing you're thinking. Otherwise you'll sign a deal thinking you're getting a Mercedes, only to discover that what's delivered is more akin to a KIA. You want to evaluate builders based upon what they have built for happy paying customers. If the builder can't show you at least three examples of that, your alarm bells should go off, as you're likely going to get baited and switched.

2) Talk to some references, for homes built here, in Baja. There are a number of operators in town who are from the States or Canada, who are trying to parlay their expertise there into a building business here. Don't fall for it. Building in Baja has about as much in common with building in the States out of sheetrock and lumber as it does with building igloos. You want to talk to references for whom the builder has successfully delivered homes in your target community, not in Michigan or Alberta. Ask the references how they liked the process. Are they happy with their home? Would they use the builder again? Do they recommend that others use him? What was the communication like? Did the quality meet their aspirations?

3) What about the quality? Walk through some homes, and look at the details, the fit and finish, the overall quality of the place. Does it seem polished and well done? Are the cabinets and closets up to par? Is the flooring well done? How about the paint? The granite? There are no perfect houses,

in Cabo, or anywhere else, however there are some well done ones that seem cleanly built and well executed. You want something as nicely done as possible at your target quality and budget range, so don't hire anyone that can't demonstrate they routinely deliver that level of quality for the money you can pay.

You need to keep one truism I've state before in mind as you go through the process here. There's no free lunch. This is an effective and competitive market. Differences in a bid group of ten percent are understandable, but differences of twenty or thirty percent aren't. The only explanation, regardless of what's tendered as the reasoning, is that you're going to be taken for a ride. And the rides generally aren't fun ones, and can occasionally be disastrous.

Perhaps one memorable way to underscore the importance of making a prudent selection is to recount a few true, verifiable stories – cautionary tales from those who didn't make wise choices. I don't offer these to scare you, but rather to underscore what can happen if the counsel in this section goes unheeded. If you prefer to skip these disturbing accounts, page ahead to the next section, where the nuts and bolts informational meat of the chapter continues.

Horror Stories

This is one of the most dramatically awful true stories I've heard since I've been here. What you need to know is that the couple in question live in Cabo most of the year, are smart and successful, and that health issues have caused their ability to focus to deteriorate over the past year or two. Those health issues are non-trivial, ultimately catastrophic, and are mentioned because it illustrates how unscrupulous the types of predators circling the waters in the region can be. It takes a very special sort of person to take advantage of folks like these – a particularly malignant sort of parasite. Keep that in mind.

It all starts out on an upbeat and promising note. They buy a lot in a large beachfront development, which doubles in value over a couple years, and they decide to build. A plan is bought off the Internet (first mistake), and modified by a local architect of questionable abilities and repute, and soon they've struck a deal with a builder recommended to them by the sales guy who sold them the lot. A Gringo, not a Mexican, BTW, lest anyone believe this is a bash against Mexicans.

Which is where the problems begin. They're never given any references they can check, other than the sales guy's assurance that this is a swell fella. The builder takes them out and shows them houses he claims to have built, but they never meet anyone he's built for, nor get to talk to anyone. But the homes look OK, and there's the assurance of the sales guy, so it seems like the builder's legit – he's been building in the area for a while, after all, and lives in the same remote area they're going to need to have the home built…so they sign up.

Months go by. They pay double the going rate for a *SEMARNAT* EIR study they don't need. They don't know any better, nor what things cost, so are none the wiser. Presumably they eventually get a building permit, because construction starts. I say presumably, because they never actually see any permit. I later discover that the building permit was never granted, but I digress.

The plans call for a home built out of foam panel, which we've discussed ad nauseum. The plan also calls for all the usual stuff – a cistern below the garage for water storage, a sewage treatment plant, etc.

They're a little apprehensive because once the deal's done, the builder starts telling them what isn't included – no pocket doors on their oceanfront home, because of "sand issues." No stone on the floors, rather cheap ceramic tile. The lowest grade aluminum windows. No sloped tile roofs, better flat, as all that tile could blow off in a hurricane. No oversized doors, as the locals can't ever get them to fit right. On and on, limitations that fatten the builder's profit at the expense of quality. But they don't know that. He seems like an honest fellow, trying to ensure that the folks make prudent choices.

Eventually the build starts, and they pay, and they pay, and they pay. Health issues command most of their bandwidth, and the builder tells them not to bother coming all the way out to see the house yet, as there's not a lot to see.

Fast forward five months, by which time most homes would have the roof on and be into the finish work. The wife drives out to look at the progress, and instead feels like she's been pole-axed in the head. There's maybe six weeks worth or construction done, all out of concrete block, not panel. The block is the cheapest money can buy. The mortar joints between the blocks violates building code. The slab that was poured is cracking apart – every room has major stress cracks, as the weight of the block caused the slab to flex, and fracture. There's no cistern under the garage – the maestro just shrugs when she asks about it. There are only a few workers on the job, who seem uninterested in the floor–to–ceiling fissures in the poorly built walls, or the myriad floor cracks. Everyone's just sort of ambling around, trying to look busy. The house isn't ready to get a roof on for at least another month. And yet the couple has already paid forty-five percent of the cash to the builder.

When confronted on the phone, the builder tells them that panel got "too expensive", so he built the house out of block instead. No consultation. No explanation. When asked about the cistern, he breezily said they would figure something out later.

Justifiably alarmed, the wife brought in several qualified experts, all of whom spent five minutes on the property before telling her she needed to stop the build, and call a lawyer. One indicated that it would probably be necessary to bulldoze it all. The other wasn't as complimentary. After an in-depth inspection took place, it was determined that the entire structure was disastrous, and wouldn't stand up for more than a few seasons. As an example, the plan called for 2 meters (7 feet) of highly-compacted dirt under the house to act as a stable platform – and what was there was a few inches. He'd basically just built the house on the sand, and completely ignored all the building code and structural plan safeguards.

When confronted, the builder turned mean, told the wife to forget about ever seeing any permits (which are her property) or plans (also hers), that he was underwater on the build (obviously a lie given the little accomplished in terms of both materials used, or labor expended), and was going to put leans on their lot, blah blah blah. To say he was abusive would be mild. They felt threatened, and their property at risk of vandalism or burglary, as this charming fellow lives out by the build location.

A little digging turned up that he hadn't applied for the building permit until a few weeks earlier (it got rejected), had told Social Security that he'd incurred almost no labor costs and thus hadn't paid any SS yet, and worst of all, hadn't drafted a contract that was legal in Mexico – thus like all his others, his claims of recourse were meaningless (as if failing to build out of the material specified, or with the features contracted for, wouldn't have been grounds for immediate termination even if there were no contractual questions).

I verified all this in a series of discussions with the couple, when they approached me after reading my Gringo Gazette columns. I went out and looked at the build. It was too late to help them with this, other than to direct them to a good bulldozing company.

The postscript is that they decided to forego building their dream home, in which they had hoped to live out their remaining time together. Lawsuits loom on the horizon, but who knows how long those will take, or what can be secured? It's a bad, bad deal all around.

Ironically, this builder is still building other homes in the same area for other lucky souls who have no idea what they've gotten into. Caveat Emptor.

Horror Stories, Part Dos

Tommy builds and sells spec homes, and has made a decent income out of it around Cabo. On his last project, Tommy employed an upcoming group that assured him they could beat everyone's prices by a wide margin, and still turn out good quality. They had a fleet of trucks, and were building around town, so he felt comfortable and tried them.

Everything went great for the first five months. No ugly surprises, and Tommy was already counting the money he'd "saved" by using them. Relatively new group, young and aggressive architect, whose favorite expression was, *"No Problema!"*

Then the honeymoon ended, and he discovered the dark side of the arrangement. Cost overruns became a monthly occurrence, and even though he'd signed a contract guaranteeing a fixed cost, the builder complained that he'd agreed to build for too little money, and was in trouble. Contract be damned, others were charging much more for decent quality, and he'd made a "mistake", and was barely going to break even. Of course, the builder didn't share this with Tommy when he'd only sunk a few hundred grand into the proposition. No, the "mistake" only surfaced once the builder had sucked seventy-five percent of the money out of him, but only had the house at about the forty-five percent stage. In other words, the builder had waited until the house couldn't be finished for what remained outstanding, and then discovered his "mistake."

That didn't go over so well with Tommy, who threatened legal action (he had an ironclad contract, and wasn't spineless). Then the builder changed tactics. Apparently a lot of the items required to complete the house had been mysteriously omitted from the list of materials included in the contract. Another "mistake." So now he was hit with big up-charges, and the explanation that those things weren't included in the "base cost." We're talking many tens and tens of thousands of up-charges.

So what's the moral of the story? If you encounter a group claiming they can build for tons less than any of the reputable builders here, guess what? Watch your wallet. A certain segment of the locals simply lowball, and then once you're well into the job and trying to manage it from thousands of miles away, they stick it to you. Even seasoned, experienced people get taken this way. It's the standard operating paradigm for a segment of the builders who've learned that it's highly effective, if totally unethical.

Unscrupulous operators promise the world, then once you're on the hook and stripping line off the reel, tighten the drag, and you have nowhere to go. It's quite calculated. They get the job to where the economics are upside down, and then put the screws to you. If you fire them or they walk, they've already pocketed most of the job's profit, and you'll wind up paying a lot more to have someone competent finish. So they don't really care. Either way, if you budgeted $1.00, you'll wind up paying $1.20-$1.50. It sucks, but it's far more common than I care to think about. And you have little recourse other than to take it.

Horror Stories, Part Tres

Another gentleman hired a builder with good references, who mocked the pricing the client had gotten from two other reputable builders, both of whom were too booked to do his home. That should have been a giveaway. This builder dismissed all other quotes as a rip-off, the locals taking advantage of vulnerable "newbies", an insult to everyone's intelligence. He quoted a great price per square foot, and was anxious to get started. The owner was delighted at his enthusiasm, and a deal was made. Crews of workers arrived, and swarmed like ants over the site. Now this was what the owner was expecting! As the first few months went by, the low price crept up – "Oh, Senor, that didn't include the retaining walls, or the cistern, or the water treatment plant, or the dirt required to create a platform. I broke out everything in my quote – I thought you understood!"

Soon, $10 more per square foot turned into $20 more, and the great deal started to turn into a great deal for the builder. Then, after a large payment to cover the domes over the dining room and entryway, and a huge increase in the cost of necessary materials, the builder appeared in a new truck, to inform the owner that his crew would be back in a few days – there was an emergency at one of the other sites that required his best guys. The owner never saw him again – or rather, he didn't see him for several months, even though every week he was told that this week would be the week when the crew returned. Ultimately, our friend hired a different contractor (who charged more realistic rates), and is suing the "good price" fellow – a lot of fun in a foreign country, where he doesn't speak much of the language, and his attorneys have explained that, while it isn't right, his experience happens all the time and isn't thought of as shocking. Oftentimes, the only asset the company has is a few trucks and tools, so chances of meaningful recovery are slim.

The project wound up costing almost forty percent more than budgeted, and he had to really stretch to finish his place.

The point to all of this is that you can really get badly snake-bit by the locals, and the gringos operating here, alike, if you aren't careful about how you go about your builder selection process. None of these stories would have happened if the counsel I set forth in these chapters had been followed by these folks. It's actually stories like these that convinced me to write this little tome – I figured if the information to avoid the worst of the mishaps was easily available and collected in one place, it would make it far more difficult for the predators to prey on the unwary.

Now that you know what not to do, let's get started on how to engage in the bid process, assuming you haven't already decided that your designer has all the necessary criteria to build your home for the price range you feel is reasonable.

Bids

You'll want to prepare a package to give to the candidates you've selected. It should contain a disk with your full plans on it, the structural plan and *memorio de calculo*, and the finish list (which can be part of the *memorio de calculo*).

Be very clear that you want the entire project quoted, with no exclusions, except the appliances, and landscaping. Those are better bid separately directly with the appliance providers, and with the landscaping companies. Most builders just mark up the landscaping services of their favorite provider, so it's counterproductive to have that in the build quote – after all, those are plants, not concrete and rebar. Different discipline.

It generally takes ten to fourteen days to generate a coherent and thorough bid. Every element has to be costed and verified, and costs shift around a lot given the currency flux and rapidly evolving global financial situation. As a builder, I can't depend on six month old pricing – it all has to be priced at the bid time.

Most bids will only be good for a period of thirty to sixty days. Reason being that any further out, and the cost of materials can change, altering the bid pricing.

What you're trying to achieve is an apples-to-apples comparison from different similarly-qualified builders. To that end, it's also best to ask for the information to be presented to you in the same manner from all parties. I tend to encourage breaking out the landfill and retaining walls portion of the bid, and then the home part of the bid as a separate series of line items. I also don't tend to dwell on semantics over differences in how square footage is addressed – I'm interested in how much the total project will cost, dirt and retaining walls, and house, including pool and terraces and driveway.

I'd also suggest that you request a breakdown by area attached to the bid so that you can assure yourself that the same material specifications are being used. I tend to want specs on block type, plumbing type, fixture allowances, carpentry type, flooring type, counter type, windows type, etc. This should all line up with your finishes description, however I've often seen bids come in where material items were changed in order to alter costs – some operators seem to correctly believe that you won't go through the bids to verify that they quoted what you asked them to quote. Specificity in the description to ensure that the quotes are the same is your friend.

If the bids are in dollars, that's easiest. If some come in with pesos, confirm the exchange rate the builder used at the time of the bid.

One observation – there's a huge difference between a bid to build a home that's an estimate, and a guaranteed not-to-exceed amount to build the home described in the plans and the *memorio de calculo*. Just as there's a world of difference between a "cost plus" approach to building a home, where the architect or builder builds the home for "cost" plus a percentage as his profit. The latter approach can work if you have a scrupulously honest builder who is accurately reporting what everything actually costs, and who hasn't worked side deals with all the suppliers to inflate costs and pocket the difference under the table.

Problem with this approach is you have no way of knowing what's actually being done – you just see *facturas* and receipts, and assume they don't have any pad. My feeling is that for most it's just an invitation to larceny. I see it as a viable way to go when currency rates are all over the map, as it really is impossible to completely guarantee costs if the currency loses thirty percent in a historic drop, however I prefer the guarantee approach with a currency peg, and an understanding that some things will be excluded from the peg if it moves more than ten percent during the life of the build – for instance, if the peso loses twenty percent against the dollar and there's a currency peg, the client owes twenty percent less dollars to generate a similar amount of pesos. That's all good, except that roughly half the stuff that goes into a house is denominated in dollars and paid for in such, thus the peg stops reflecting a hedge for the builder after a certain point and becomes unworkable.

In challenging times it's best to have an agreement that allows everyone to be reasonable to reflect unpredictable volatility – no builder will build a house if it winds up costing him to do so due to currency flux, so as a client you need to acknowledge that simple reality. It's your house, and you aren't going to give the builder a twenty percent bonus if it winds up being worth a hundred percent more than you paid him for it by the end of the deal, so he's not going to invest his money to build your house. The best agreements are ones that are reasonable, so one needs to strive for agreements where everyone's needs are met.

It used to be that this issue was pretty simple – the peso would stay in a two percent or so range vis a vis the dollar, thus it wasn't a big deal. You just denominated the deal in either pesos, or dollars, and went on your way. In 2008, however, we saw the dollar fluctuate from 11.7 to 9.8 to 14.4 within a six month period or so. No builder can predict once-a-century currency volatility, nor can any contract or agreement bind a builder to lose money building your house – there isn't a court in the land that would enforce it. So until things become more stable and find a new range, be prepared for a challenging time on the currency issue.

Anyway, once you have your bids back from the builders you have qualified as suitable candidates, you can compare what they bid to what you asked them to bid, and assuming they're compliant, can select a builder and move forward.

Structuring a Deal

You have your bids, and after much discussion and thought, you've selected your builder. So how do you go about structuring a deal that you can live with, that protects you, and that spells out necessary criteria, like schedule, payment terms, warranty, late penalties, and the host of protections that a good agreement should contain?

Most builders will have a contract that calls out all of this, however you can review the following suggested inclusions to confirm that all the requisites are present.

Language, and Governing Law

To be one hundred percent legal, a contract in Mexico needs to be written in both English and Spanish, or just Spanish. English language contracts aren't valid here, although it's possible to have one translated after the fact and likely have it stand up in court. But it's way easier to just have the contract done in both languages around contract signing time, keeping everything simple.

Governing law should be Mexican law, and venue should be in San Jose Del Cabo, or Cabo San Lucas, BCS.

Project Definition

Any agreement should have the project scope defined. That means that there should be at least a paragraph describing the size of the project, the key features of the house, the lot it's going to be built on, and any other information germane to the project. I also like to see an addendum showing a much more granular list of all features and finishes called out, and attached as a part of the agreement, so it can be referred back to should any confusion arise over the course of the build. Memory is a strange thing – as you go through a project for a year, and discuss and re-discuss myriad possibilities and choices, it can become jumbled together, and either you or your builder can confuse what was agreed to in the contract, with something discussed post hoc.

I generally create five to six pages of project definition, that covers everything from the types of toilets, to the type of AC, to the size and type of flooring, to carpentry details, to paint type, wiring type, building material type, plaster thickness, plumbing material, glass and window frame type, roofing material, decking material, and allowances for every aspect of the home build – doorknobs, faucets, showers, garage door, etc. etc.

I do this so that it's crystal clear what the project is going to contain, and so that it's obvious what's included, and what's a change order. I have found that being reasonable after the fact is key, and a well defined list is key to keeping everyone reasonable. As I've mentioned before, if it isn't on the plan or in this sort of list, it isn't in the bid, so this gives clients a chance to confirm that everything is indeed included. It isn't that hard to do, as the *memorio* and the plan will generally contain all the info I need.

Additionally, you want articulated what isn't included in the build agreement – for instance, if landscaping is a separate deal, it should exclude that specifically. Same for appliances, or any other mutually-agreed-upon exclusions.

You'll also want some sort of a statement indicating that you own the lot free and clear, and that the builder will take care of whatever permits are necessary – but payment for those permits should be clearly defined. Most have the client pay for the building permit and any requisite homeowner's association permits, as there's no way to know exactly how much those will run up front – at least not the building permit. Having said that, building permits generally cost one percent of the total construction cost, or thereabouts.

Now, here again is an area where you can get taken. Oftentimes, a builder will try to understate the construction costs for the purposes of obtaining a cheaper permit. All well and good, however the tax authority will use that permit to define the value of the home – which will dictate the capital gains tax amount due when you sell it. So the lower the amount, the greater the tax owed, as tax is due on the difference between the lot cost plus the construction cost, and the sale price. So if you have a lot you paid $400,000 for, and construction you paid $1 million for, and it's listed as $500,000 of construction, you would only get $900,000 of credit for tax purposes on the sale, as opposed to $1.4 million of true value. Sell the house for $2 million, and you can see that by understating the building permit amount to save a few grand, you just cost yourself tens of thousands in taxes due. Not a good bet. My advice is always to stay on the up and up. It will work better for you in the long run.

There also should be some sort of a disclaimer or clarification about soil conditions, as the builder has no way of knowing what's under your lot – hidden springs, oil, faults, quicksand a hundred feet down, etc. No builder will take responsibility for soil condition or pre-existing conditions, and it's your lot, so you get to be responsible. This is why I advise you to get a United States geologist to do soil samples if you're concerned about the composition of the lot. I'm not talking about the dirt platform or the landfill the builder brings in – that's the builder's responsibility. I'm talking about the lot as it exists prior to anything being done.

Title, Taxes, Social Security

A good agreement will also require proof of title before the builder starts. They'll need this to get you the building permit, so it should be stated as a responsibility of the client. What you'll need is a copy of your *Fideicomiso* to be submitted to *Obras Publicas* – Public Works, the department that issues the building permit. A word of counsel here, BTW – don't view things like the *SEMARNAT* permit or a building permit as optional. They're mandatory, and you'll be fined big if you don't have them (remember again that *SEMARNAT* isn't going to be required in established developments, just for beachfront or random lots outside of developments). Same for ecology permits for foliage. You need all these before you start, with the building permit OK in "applied for" status for the first few weeks of the build, but no more.

You'll also need to provide proof that you paid your property taxes before you can get a building permit, so most agreements will have verbiage to that effect as well.

Social Security is a big deal in Mexico, and the builder needs to pay it, monthly, with no shenanigans, or you, the owner, will be in jeopardy. The agreement should spell out who's responsible for paying social security and workers compensation – typically, the builder. Many will put it in your name, to further eliminate claims down the road that your SS wasn't paid, however the builder should be writing the checks. That's part of the cost of building, and usually the builder's responsibility. But spell it out. Remember, this contract is your lifeline should you, or the builder, get hit by a bus. If it isn't spelled out, it's up for grabs, which you want to avoid to the extent that it's avoidable.

Change Orders

There should be some sort of language covering the change order policy, so that it's in black and white. This is for both your, and the builder's, protection. As discussed, change orders introduce cost that wasn't in the bid, and also introduce delays (due to having to make the changes instead of plowing ahead with the home as bid), thus they have an effect both on the final cost of the home, as well as the finish date. I will do change orders, in writing, periodically as the changes mount up. I find most projects have anywhere from three change orders, to ten, with a group of modifications on each CO. They're due and payable when issued, as the changes have to be paid for at that time, and thus aren't built into the payment scheme.

Many builders will accumulate many "while you're at it" changes, and then you'll be hit with a change order toward the end of the build. That can amount to many tens of thousands of dollars, and can be a huge shock, as you weren't calculating each change as you went. My philosophy is that it's more transparent and palatable to issue periodic COs so that the client can have a sense of how they're doing, rather than hitting them with a lump sum at the end. There's no argument that you'll owe the money – you asked for the changes, and the builder made them, so you need to pay for them – however I tend to think that people appreciate a running tally, as they might make different choices if they're keenly aware of the costs being introduced.

Remember from the bid discussion that builders bid what's on the plan, not what may be needed on the plan at a later date (or introduced halfway through). Adding things, modifying things, eliminating or moving things, all cost money and cause delays. For instance, if you decide to add a window, or move a light fixture, elves don't do those things – workers do. Workers who were assigned on the schedule to complete some other task have to stop what they're doing, and then add the window or move the fixture. After they're done, they can then resume whatever they were supposed to be doing. That's how change orders introduce delays – there isn't an infinite crew base on a project to draw upon and scale according to what changes are introduced. There's typically a *Maestro* and fifteen to twenty workers to do it all. If three of those workers have to be taken off task A to do change B, task A gets delayed that amount. And the cost to redirect them is an additional cost, due to whatever new materials are required, as well as for their time to complete the change.

There's no right or wrong way to handle change orders, however you want whatever the manner that will be used to be articulated in writing.

Schedule and Payment Scheme

This is probably the single most important aspect of the contract, as it defines how long it will take to build your house, as well as how the moneys are to be broken down and paid.

I will say up front that different builders will take different durations to finish a house. While there are no hard and fast rules, I can give you some rules of thumb to use when negotiating your project.

My average size home is between forty-four hundred and six thousand square feet. It will generally take me a year to complete a home of this size, assuming not too many change orders, and reasonable storm season – we lose a week or so total to storms, not much more. That's in addition to the time it takes to create the platform and deal with landfill and retaining walls. Sometimes I get homes done quicker, occasionally, on larger homes, it takes me a bit longer as there's more complexity and detail to contend with. But average is twelve months. Thus, my contract allows for twelve months of payments, with the twelfth and final due upon occupancy or completion walkthrough, whichever occurs first.

I will usually get a down-stroke when the contract is signed, and will use that first payment to lock in key commodities that pose the most risk of rising in price – usually concrete and steel. Then, I will schedule out eleven payments, essentially financing the rest of the home build.

Some prefer to also associate key payments to milestones – completion of *obra negra*, completion of flooring, etc. One can do that as well, or do a hybrid where one has both monthly payments, as well as sanity stops at critical percentages (such as the fifth payment to occur only assuming that *obra negra* is completed). There's no fixed way to do all this, although I have found that my payment scheme roughly tracks progress, thus works well for me.

Sometimes it appears that the client is paid a little ahead of actual progress. However that's also usually at a point where substantial amounts have been laid out for deposits on key items like flooring, or AC, or carpentry and windows, thus the money has been invested in items to be delivered later. I have yet to build a home where it was an issue to complete the home given this payment scheme, so I've stuck with it, with only small variations.

The key here is that you want a payment mechanism that allows you to track progress, and where you don't get too far ahead on the money versus what's actually been built. At fifty percent complete, you want to be around fifty percent or so paid. At eighty percent paid, you want to be eighty percent done. And so on. Whether you link it to milestones, or by the month, the idea is to pay out the money in measured tranches commensurate with actual progress.

You also want to establish a schedule, wherein you have a rough timeline of how long it's going to take to build your home. There should be a penalty clause to protect you should it run late, such as X number of dollars for every working day over the target date the project runs – after taking into account change order latency, and acts of God – storm delays, seismic events, etc. More on that in the next section.

I tell folks to expect some delays, and brace themselves for them, as more than ninety percent of the homes here run late. That's just the way it works, for whatever reason. However, the objective is to limit any tardiness, and to ensure that your builder can finish the project.

And now for the most important (and hated by my peers) advice I can tender: Never pay the final payment until the house is done. That's your holdout to get it finished – don't give it up until you have taken occupancy. In some instances, I've seen builders ask for and get fifty percent of the final payment in order to finish the home (in situations where the builder underestimated the cost to build the house, and actually needs the money to get it done), however once the final payment is completely paid, that's it except for warranty repairs.

By the same token, it's unreasonable to hold up the final payment if the home is completed and you're moved in, but you have a punch-list of items you want fixed or done over. Those are warranty repairs, not items to complete the house. You need to distinguish between warranty work and completion of the house work. More on that in the next chapters, with a brief description of warranty clauses to follow.

Late Fees

It is now standard fare in agreements here to have some sort of penalty clause that costs the builder should he run late. That's reasonable, as time is money, and if the build time articulated in the contract is reasonable and yet the builder runs over, and the latency isn't due to change orders or acts of God, he should compensate you for running late. The amount is subject to negotiation, but I have seen everything from a hundred dollars to two hundred dollars a working day, based upon the total contract value. Generally, for a sub-million or million dollar contract, a hundred dollars is reasonable, and when you're up in the couple million, two hundred dollars a day is reasonable. The key here isn't to drive the builder into the poorhouse, but rather to create pressure to finish the house as close to on time as possible.

Again, you have to take into account any latency introduced due to change orders, as they can introduce months of delays if they're non-trivial. But that, and things like hurricanes, should be the only outs.

By the same token, there should also be a penalty for you, the client, if you don't pay on time, as that generally imposes a hardship on the builder, who is using your payment stream to build your house. I've seen many variations for this, but the penalty has to be reasonable.

Warranty

Hopefully, you've selected a builder whose work won't require much warranty activity after the first round of acceptance touch-ups and repairs. I say this because if the home is built competently, most of the warranty work will take place in the thirty days following acceptance, as your punch-list of corrections and repairs necessary is handed over and a pick-up crew is dispatched to whip out the repairs. Still, roofs have been known to leak, wiring to short out, plumbing to leak, pools to leak. That's why a warranty from a reputable builder is essential – most give a one year warranty, however warranty support varies from responsive, to dismal. Still, you need to get it in writing, and what you want is an agreement to repair or replace any defects in materials or workmanship for a period of one year from the time the home is handed over or occupied.

Those are the basics of the agreement. Review your contract to ensure it has all these elements spelled out in a manner that can serve as the basis of conflict resolution in court, should it all hit the fan. Most likely, if you've followed the counsel in these pages to this point, you won't really need to hammer on any of these clauses, as your builder will do the right thing, however it's nice to have things clarified in writing should he decide not to.

Checklist

- Identify target candidate builders. Look at their work. Talk to references. Consider homes in your target quality and price range, not homes double the price. You want to understand what you'll get for the money you've budgeted, not homes out of your range.

- Qualify the candidates.

- Shop your bid package. Include plans, *memorio de calculo*, and finishes list.

- Vet the bid responses. Confirm apples to apples, and like materials.

- Review contracts for key areas. Governing law, project description, title confirmation, SS and permit disposition, schedule and payment scheme, penalty clauses, warranty coverage.

Chapter 5 – Platform and Obra Negra, Timeline

Overview

You've qualified a builder and worked out a deal you can live with, having taken care to ensure that your agreement is definitive, complete, and contains all the requisites discussed in the last chapter. Money's changed hands, and you've made the important transition from *planning* a house, to *building* a house.

Congratulations. A lot of hard work and perseverance has resulted in a plan you're more than somewhat familiar with, which you understand and like, and which reflects your unique set of tastes, style, and needs. Now it's going to make the leap from lines on a piece of paper, to an actual structure manifest in the physical world.

The purpose of this chapter is to walk you through important phases in the permit process, landfill/excavation process, and in the first major portion of the home's construction – what's referred to as *Obra negra*.

Obra negra describes the point where the walls are up and the roof's on, conduit is run, along with plumbing, and everything looks grey – the structure is done, but the finishes haven't gone in yet. It's before the plaster starts, but after the roof's poured.

The next chapter will cover the second portion of the home's construction, which are the finishes – plaster, roof tile, windows, flooring, carpentry, etc. This chapter will concentrate on a blow by blow description of what to expect, and what to watch out for, from the time you break ground to the point you're done with *obra negra*.

Pulling Permits and Breaking Ground

Your builder will take your identification, a full set of stamped plans (if in a development that requires a stamp certifying that it has been approved by the homeowner's architectural review board), the structural plan, and the *memorio de calculo* to *Obras Publicas* to get your building permit. *Obras Publicas* is the Department of Public Works.

Issuance of the permit can take two weeks to a month or more, depending upon the time of year, and the workload. In Mexico, around the Christmas holidays, everything pretty much shuts down from December fifteenth or so to January tenth, mas o menos, so at that time of the year it can take even longer.

Prior to getting the building permit, your builder will have the Ecology Department come out, and they'll take an inventory of the flora on your lot, and issue a permit after you've agreed to pay the fee they calculate clearing your lot will require – usually it's X number of trees, costing Y dollars per tree. The builder will go out and buy the trees, and the permit will be issued, at which point you can clear the lot. Sometimes Ecology will also tag protected species of cactus or trees, which must be moved to a safe place and replaced on the lot once construction is completed. That's more common in developments like Puerto Los Cabos, which has the capability of storing cactus in protected areas.

A word of warning. Clearing your lot before you have the ecology permit is a really bad idea, a no-no in the eyes of the ecology guys. You'll open yourself up to large fines if you do so. They've figured out this is a revenue generator for them, so they actually pay attention. You really don't want to test their vigilance on this – when there's money on the table, they'll make the effort to monitor building permits and check to verify they got their pound of flesh before it was issued. Don't push the envelope on this; it will come back to bite you.

Once you have the permit, you can clear the lot, which generally entails razing it. Often, clients will request that certain plants or cactus be saved or remain untouched, however the truth is that when the backhoe comes onto the lot, it scrapes it clean. It's a blunt instrument, not a razor, so understand that unless you've arranged to have cherished or protected vegetation transplanted elsewhere, they'll likely be flattened. That's the truth, and there's little chance of fighting it, so save your energy for battles you can win.

At the point it's cleared, the fun starts. If it's an uphill lot, excavation will begin, to dig out the portion of the ground that will contain the home's platform and foundation. If a flat lot, the dirt will start getting trucked in to create the platform. If a downhill slope lot, work will start on the retaining walls that will keep the dirt that later arrives from sliding down the hill.

(IMPORTANT *SEMARNAT* NOTE: If your lot is on a beachfront, or isn't in an established development where the developer got a blanket *SEMARNAT* permit for the community, you'll need to get an Environmental Impact Study (EIR) done, and then submit that to *SEMARNAT* for a permit. Getting the permit can take ninety days, and in some cases, considerably longer. It also can cost a decent chunk of change to obtain. It's not optional, and starting construction without the *SEMARNAT* permit can lead to large fines. Your builder should know about all this, but it doesn't hurt to ask to confirm he's done his homework.)

The platform will be of varying thickness, depending upon what the underlying terrain is like. Generally speaking, it will be up to a meter or so of compacted dirt. Compaction is achieved by bringing in suitable soil, and then laying it down a few inches at a time, while rolling over it with a steam roller and wetting it down with water. This process will go on for days, or weeks, until your platform is done – done being compacted to a target of ninety-five percent proctor (a measurement of density and compaction).

Different terrain will require different platform thicknesses, with sand requiring the most – two meters or so of platform, if you want to have a safe and durable structure. And all that dirt costs. The brown, sedimentary stuff isn't cheap. Dirt may be free, but compacting and transporting dirt isn't. Those courteous drivers and pristinely-maintained trucks cost a lot. No kidding. A truck full can easily run from $130 to $200+, depending upon how far the dirt needs to travel, and including compaction. Hopefully by now you understand what it's going to cost to build the platform, as you should have gotten the pricing as part of your bid, however it can still be astounding to see the bills come in for a platform.

Once the platform's formed, most of the time you'll start on retaining walls (assuming it isn't a down slope lot, where the walls go in first). The number and thickness shouldn't be a surprise, as they should be on your plan, however sometimes a wall or two gets left off. They shouldn't, but it's been known to happen. I've actually seen homes where the owners invited me over to find out what would keep the side of their house from eroding and washing away in the first hurricane – and I've seen the expression on their face when I told them there was nothing to stop that, and that they were going to need some retaining walls (at a significant cost).

As I've repeatedly indicated, an unfortunate truth is that if it isn't on the plan, it isn't in the bid, and their designer hadn't contemplated how to keep the side of the house from eroding away – could be it wasn't even an issue when the plan was drawn, as the lot hadn't been cleared and the totality of the terrain wasn't known. But at the end of the day, the client would need to cough up the cash to build the requisite walls, as it was their house they were protecting. The builder wasn't a mind reader, and thus couldn't foresee what would be required once the lot was cleared, and neither was the designer. While it's unfortunate, these things can and do occur, and not necessarily due to any larceny or incompetence. It's just one of the responsibilities of building a home – you have to be prepared for the unexpected.

Back to the actual retaining walls, though. Smaller walls will be built out of eight inch block and reinforced with rebar, whereas anything of real significance will be poured concrete and rebar, or natural stone and concrete.

Labor

At this point, I should also describe the composition of the crew that will be building your home through the end of *obra negra*. There will be a *Maestro*, who is the foreman on the ground, and the laborers. The *Maestro* is in charge of the day-to-day supervision of the crew, and ensures that the plan is being followed and that good techniques are being used. Above him will be an engineer who is also the DRO – the *Director Responsible for the Obra* – as well as an architect. The number of times that the DRO will actually be at the site will vary depending upon the DRO. Ditto for the architect.

The guy who is actually going to have the most impact on the quality of the build at this stage is the *Maestro*, who's the one standing in the sun ten hours a day ensuring that the labor is working efficiently, safely, and intelligently. If he has a little drinking problem, or is too chummy with his crew, or is sloppy or inattentive, you could have real problems.

I keep the same *Maestros* from job to job, as once you find one that's trustworthy and knows his craft, you want to keep him. Most other higher quality builders do the same. I've seen some companies operate differently, where one group comes in and puts up the *obra negra*, and then a different *Maestro* shows up to finish the home. That can work if the two are accustomed to working together. It's true that finishes require a different skill-set than *obra negra*, however a good *Maestro* should have both finish and *obra negra* experience, and should be able to run the project from beginning to end.

The Crew

One of the most gratifying experiences I know is watching a piece of barren dirt transformed into a home. It's one of the reasons I build houses. I'm constantly in awe of the process of creating something from nothing, and am fond of saying that destruction is easy, construction is hard – it takes a day to bulldoze a house, but a year to build one.

Part of the awe is watching the crews get out of the backs of pickups and vans every morning, equipped with nothing more than what they can carry in a bucket or fit in an old tool belt. Yet these workers erect everything from custom luxury homes, to condo high-rises, using worn hammers, and chisels, and steel bars. Absent are the sophisticated power tools that are ubiquitous on American jobs. Everywhere in Baja, just after dawn, construction crews are building the region with little more than their bare hands. Yet the level of fit and finish can be surprisingly high, as skills honed over decades are brought to bear, and pride of craftsmanship is sometimes the only badge of honor available.

The *Maestro's* abilities will ultimately dictate the quality of the crew, as the better *Maestros* seek out the better craftsmen. Your *Maestro* is the lynchpin of your home's ultimate finish, so it can pay to spend some time at the site watching how he works with his men, and how involved he is in the process. That will tell you a world about how nice the home is likely to be.

When you're checking on the quality of the build, pay attention to how the *Maestro* interacts with his crew. A good one will command respect, and be involved in every aspect of the build. He isn't there to be buddies, or make friends, he's there to build a home, which is what he's likely done for the last twenty years or so. When you're evaluating your build, you should also evaluate your *Maestro*, and if you have concerns, raise them with your builder sooner rather than later.

Preparing the Slab

Once the retaining walls are in, you're ready to get started on construction of the house.

This can be a bit anti-climactic, as one of the first things that needs to happen is the bending of rebar. For weeks, men will bend rebar using pipe levers and a table, and form the steel that will go into the footers and the structural columns. Footers, for those new to this, are the concrete bases/anchors that go into the ground along the edge of the slab and beneath the walls.

The crew will dig trenches along a chalk outline that represents the walls of the house, including the interior walls. This is an important point in the construction for you, the client, as it will be the first time in the physical world that you'll get a sense of the actual space of the home on the actual lot. It's a good idea to show up when they chalk out the home, because if you have any last minute thoughts that an area is too small or that a wall should be pushed out, this is when you should do it, as it's way cheaper to modify a plan when it's only chalk, as opposed to concrete and rebar. I try to get my clients to come down when we're at this stage if at all possible for this reason. Several times I've enlarged whole sections of a house at this stage, as the clients recognize that what was drawn was insufficient to achieve the effect they want.

What can happen is that in the battle to save money on square footage, clients can opt to make areas smaller than I would recommend. I have a lot of experience with designing spaces, and I will try to get things laid out in what I believe is an optimum way, but sometimes the imperative of cost reduction wins out over design sensibility. Clients will insist that they don't want to pay a dime more than they have to, which is understandable, and choose to go for smaller areas where they think they can. What can happen is that once they stand on the lot and see the chalk marks of the walls, they realize I wasn't trying to pump up the size just to get more money out of them, but rather that the space really needed to be larger to get the intended effect – for the good of the house, and ultimately the client. At that point, they get it, and will usually agree that the wall or area needs to be enlarged – and again, at that point it's just a day's redraw and some additional structural calculation, and the additional expense of more flooring, more roof, more plaster.

Back to the chalk. You're standing on your lot, and there are a network of these white lines on your platform, representing your home. It's a good time to confirm with yourself that it's what you want, in terms of all spaces. Within a few days, the crew will have dug all the trenches along the wall lines, in preparation of laying the rebar into the trenches (in preparation for pouring the footers with concrete), and that has a different effect than chalk.

It can seem counterintuitive that the laborers dig out a platform that was just created at such great expense, but that's how they do it. As described, they'll create a series of trenches, which will hold the footers. Then they put rebar into the trenches, and the plumbers and electricians will come in and run the water pipes, the drain and sewer lines, and the conduit. This process, from the time they start cutting trenches to when the rebar is in place, along with the plumbing and conduit, will take about three weeks to a month. Depends on the size of the house – smaller homes it might take two and a half weeks, larger homes a month.

Then in come the concrete trucks. In one day, they'll pour several truckloads of cement, creating the slab. This assumes that your builder is using a standard technique for building with block. If he's using "post and beam" technique, he will pour foundations for the columns, and move directly to creating the structural columns and the cross beams, creating the slab whenever he chooses, as in that technique, the slab isn't structural. In standard technique it is. Either way, at this point you need to know some things about concrete, and building in Baja. The most important thing is that the strength of the concrete, the PSI, depends upon the ratio of cement to sand. More sand, lower PSI.

There are plenty of horror stories about retaining walls, bridges, and whole structures collapsing due to inadequate PSI concrete being used. Apparently it's not unknown for concrete guys to increase their profit margin by mixing in more sand than is called for, saving bucks on cement, but also endangering your build. The way I usually solve this is to let the concrete guys know I am going to have the concrete tested, which I do, on both concrete pours as well as when buying block. If they know they're going to be liable if they don't deliver what was paid for, it keeps everyone honest.

I'm not saying that the concrete companies are all crooks, because they aren't, but human nature is to save money where one can, and if you don't know the difference, hey, it's a tough world. This will also be a concern when your crew is mixing smaller batches of concrete by mixing sand and cement onsite. A sack of cement in the trunk of a car at the end of the day's build can translate to beer money for the evening, and it isn't unheard of for enterprising crews operating with less than vigilant supervision to mix in a tad more sand, in order to "save" a bag or two of cement. There's no way for you to know if that's going on, however the *Maestro* should be watching for it.

Somewhere in the above slab prep and pour process, the builder will also dig a big hole in the ground for the cistern, line it with waterproofed block reinforced with rebar, and then pour the top slab for the cistern.

Which introduces a common question for folks who have never lived here, which is, "Why bother with a cistern when we're hooked up to city water?"

As touched upon in earlier chapters, water from the city can be sporadic, or non-existent after a big storm. Sometimes for weeks. And during the summer, it can just shut off for days at a time for no apparent reason. Occasionally, something bad can happen up the line, and water is disrupted indefinitely. At which point you need to truck water in, which isn't the end of the world…. but having no water for weeks at a time is bad. Very bad. It's imprudent and just unsound to design and build a home in Baja without a cistern, and most builders will tell you the same. Any money you save by not putting one in won't be worth the aggravation when the waterline stops delivering.

Another common question is, how does the water get from the cistern to the taps? In the United States and Canada, you're hooked up to the pressure system from the city, so it's not your issue. Here, you need a hydraulic pump with a pressure tank – you supply your own pressure, just as with a boat. City water dumps into the cistern, a float shutoff valve shuts off the inflow once the cistern is full, and your hydro pump sucks water in from the cistern, and then maintains a certain pressure so that water can get to the taps at reasonable pressure.

Most here opt to install a UV water purification system at the pump area, to kill ninety-nine percent of the organisms that can make you sick should you drink unpurified water. I've seen a number of them, and they all rely on the same premise – water flows through a large SS cylinder, where it's exposed to high intensity ultraviolet light, which kills the organisms in the water, rendering it safe to drink. It's relatively inexpensive, and will destroy everything I can think of around here except for cryptosporidium, which UV doesn't affect. In addition to the pump and tank and UV, you'll also need an inline filter, which needs to be changed out periodically. That filter is for sediment and crud that gets sucked in from the cistern. Most change out the filters every six months or so.

Walls

But back to the story of the slab. Once it's poured, the walls can start going up. This is an exciting time in the life of the build, as everything seems to happen pretty fast – where just a few weeks before there was nothing but dirt, now a house appears. Walls go up, the concrete and rebar structural columns are poured, and the plumbing and conduit is run through the block, which can seem really primitive and chaotic to the uninitiated. What happens is that groups of men with hammers and chisels dig trenches in the block walls, which the various pipes fit into. Unlike with sheetrock construction, there really is no way to get a pipe or electric run up a wall but to bust out the concrete where it's going to go.

This is probably a good time to discuss exactly what you're looking at as the walls go up, so you can gauge for yourself whether the *obra negra* is being done competently. First off, Baja has a building code, which calls for mortar joints in concrete block walls to not exceed one inch, or 2.5 cm. This is because mortar has different properties than concrete block, in that it isn't nearly as strong, thus in an earthquake larger joints can give way, causing the walls to come tumbling down. It's relatively easy to look at your walls, and measure the mortar joints. If they're all, or even mostly, under an inch, good for you. If there a lot of joints with more than an inch, you likely have a problem, regardless of any assurances you get from your builder.

Another item to understand is that the block walls don't really have any structural properties. The structural part of the house is the network of structural beams and columns, the skeleton of the home. What you put between the beams and columns is somewhat immaterial – block, Styrofoam, autoclave aerated concrete, sheetrock, whatever. It's the columns and beams that hold the thing up. Still, you need to watch your block quality and mortar joints because those are going to support items like your windows, and cheap block will crack apart over time, causing ongoing maintenance headaches for you. And as previously mentioned, in seismic areas, you need the heavy block walls to stand up in a good shake, not break apart due to lousy quality or too much mortar.

While we are talking windows and doors and walls, you should also have rebar and concrete reinforcements at the bases of all windows, as well as on either side of doors, as well as overhead in the doorways. That's so that they don't crack over time, but also so in an earthquake you can stand in a doorway for protection, without having the doorway collapse on you. If your *obra negra* doesn't have these support structures built into the windows and doorways, you have a problem. Pay attention when you walk through your *obra negra*, and confirm that the requisite structural elements are there.

This is also the stage where you might want to try the block drop, as a quick and dirty mechanism to verify the integrity of the cinder block being used. As described previously, you pick up a concrete block off the pile that has been delivered, and you hold it at chest height, and then drop it onto dirt – not asphalt or concrete, dirt – taking care to miss your feet. If it's decent block, it will remain intact. If it's questionable or bad block, it will break apart into a bunch of pieces. The worst sort of junk block will actually more crumble apart than break apart. Again, this is because there's very little cement, and way too much sand. Another easy way to tell whether the block is acceptable is to just eyeball it – good block will seem tightly adhered, and very uniform, with sharp edges.

Bad block will look very grainy or porous, almost like heavy grit held together with cement water, which is sort of what it is. The edges will be crumbly and uneven, and it will look, well, junky. I only use two suppliers for block who I've vetted over the years as delivering consistently high quality. One way unscrupulous builders will save money is by buying inferior block, figuring you'll never be the wiser. Now you're armed with enough info to know the difference, which will hopefully improve the general quality of building around here as this little book circulates and the shifty understand that their secrets are out of the bag.

You also might want to eyeball the plumbing and electric, to verify that they appear in the places you wanted them. Don't be a pest, but do recognize that the more eyes on a project to catch SNAFUs, the more likely the end result will be a good one. Try not to fall into the trap of becoming adversarial with your builder – again, trust, but verify. Sometimes there will be things you catch if you're watching closely that your builder won't at that stage, which will save everyone time, as it costs more to fix things once the finishes are almost done than in *obra negra*. At the end of the day, stuff happens, and your builder has got enough experience to roll with it and do on-the-fly fixes and corrections, however the more items that can be verified as being correct at every stage, the less work required at the end of the job, which everyone will be thankful for.

Beyond these easily verified elements, there isn't a lot of vigilance required from you as a client. The walls go up, the conduit and plumbing go in, and the roof or first floor ceiling get prepared (if multi-story), which uses a different technique than for the slab. Wood, and lots of it, will appear at the site, and wood beams will pepper the construction supporting plywood above, which in turn will hold up the concrete when it gets poured. A network of yet more fabricated rebar beams will be laid in a grid pattern, and in each grid a thick Styrofoam block will get laid. Basically, the rebar grid is the support for the roof or second floor, and will receive the next pour of concrete, and the Styrofoam blocks act as insulation for the roof, or between floors. Heat rises, and thermal transfer is minimized if you have a six inch wall of Styrofoam between floors or under the roof tile, thus the logic of the approach.

Once the roof or second floor is poured, the process of putting walls up is either repeated, or you're done with the basic structure. At this point, most builders will put the exterior coating of mortar on the house, and prepare the interior for *yeso* (plaster).

You should be consulted as to the amount of texture the exterior finish has, given that different finishes have different appeal and style. I've found that the more gritty finishes can look appealing on contemporary structures, as well as on the classical/Mediterranean style homes. The general rule of thumb is that the finer the grain of the finish, the more likely it is to show imperfections. And all hand-made structures will have imperfections. At the end of the day, I tend to ask clients, "How many of them do you want to see?" That's a very pragmatic but truthful way of approaching the choice, and one you should consider. There are multi-million dollar homes all over Cabo with exteriors that feature ripples and cut-ins on the exterior mortar. It's one of the delights of working in concrete. And lest the synthetic folks get all cocky, I've seen just as "unique" looking finishes on virtually all the panel homes I've ever seen. Choose your exterior finish with a certain degree of pragmatism, and you'll be fine.

So the structure is up, the roof is poured, and the exterior mortar is applied.

That's *obra negra*.

The whole process will take anywhere from ten to sixteen weeks, depending upon the house size and the size of the crew being used. Generally speaking, *obra negra* takes forty percent or so of the time it will take to build the house, sometimes thirty-five percent, sometimes forty-five percent. If you're on a one year timeline from the time the platform is ready, you should be finished with *obra negra* by month number four, at the latest. Different builders use different techniques, and I've used post and beam technique on some structures to shave *obra negra* down to ten or eleven weeks on multi-story builds, however those are the rough timeframes it should take. By this stage, you also may have a big hole in the ground dug where your pool will go (assuming you have one), however most of the terraces and decks and whatnot won't have gone in yet, nor will the driveway or surrounding groundwork.

Obra negra is the building of the house to the point where the roof is on and the mortar is on the exterior, and the cistern is in and the electric junction boxes are in place. The rest of the build, and the art, is in the finishes, which are covered in the next chapter.

Timeline

What follows is a simplified description of the stages involved in building a home here, and a rough idea of how long things take.

1. Run the design past the HOA for approval or changes. This is part of the design phase, and shouldn't start the clock yet on the construction timeline.

2. Obtain building permits, and ecological approval. This shouldn't go into the timeline as part of the construction time, as builders can't control government work. This can take a week or two, or a month or two – longer on beach lots.

3. Clear the lot, and remove debris and scrub. Prep for landfill.

4. Dig trenches for retaining wall footings. Pour footings. Build retaining walls.

5. Move landfill onto lot after wall cures. This can take a few days, or a few weeks. Depends on how many truckloads of dirt are required. Once dirt is on lot, compact the fill (actually in stages, but let's not get too picky) and create construction platform.

6. <u>Clock Starts On Home Build</u>. Chalk out footprint. Dig trenches for footings. Also dig pool, and water storage area. Install sewage treatment plant in ground.

7. Pour foundation footings. Allow time to cure, then pour foundation slab. Plumbing and wire runs have also been laid at this stage.

8. Build house support frame from concrete and rebar. At this point, the structure can look like a big frame skeleton made out of concrete, The walls fill the gaps. That frame is the backbone of the house, the actual structural support.

9. Fill in the frame with concrete block/other material. The walls go up at this phase. Sometimes walls will go up, with support columns poured as they go along. Both are valid techniques.

10. Walls are up, prep ceiling/2nd floor. Bring in foam blocks, lay them, and pour concrete over them. Voila, second floor ready to build.

11. Repeat support frame at second level. Block in the walls. Presto, second floor done.

12. Prep roof for construction. Frame off with wood, lay foam blocks, pour concrete. Roof poured, *obra negra* now ninety percent complete.

13. Finish exterior rough finish in concrete.

At this point you've completed the rough build (*obra negra*) on the structure. Start to finish this will run about three to four months.

14. Start on interior. Plaster walls, install AC ducts. Finish ceilings at end of this phase. Clean up floors. Wood supports will be left in place to hold up roof and second floor while concrete cures. Don't worry, the house will stay up once they're gone.

15. Flooring starts, and Carpentry gets ordered. This usually takes months. You can't rush a carpenter. It's like making a baby, takes the same amount of time regardless of how many are trying. Relax. Let them get it right. Sliding doors go in, so do windows. The roof tiles will go on during this period, as well as brick domes. Then the housepainters do their deed. Exterior finish fixes should be done by now.

16. Carpentry boxes arrive. Deck surfaces go in, as do terrace surfaces. Counters go atop the boxes. AC units and hydro-pumps should be in by now, along with water heaters. Ironwork should also be installed, or in-process.

17. Appliances go in. Flooring finished. Carpentry largely done. Fixtures in. Exterior touches like pool area, pool, sidewalks, driveway done. Bolt on the hurricane shutters. Gotta protect all that interior now.

18. End stage, touchup work. Refine finishes, coordinate with landscapers, who will work about a week or two, and will install sprinklers and plants. Inspect for deficiencies, correct any flaws.

19. Final walkthrough, give owner keys. You just built a home in Baja.

Start to finish, I say allow a month or so for the site prep and foundations, four months for the rough (at most), eight or so for the finish work. It can always take longer, but really shouldn't. Still, if it runs a month or two over, better to get the fine details right than to freak out and rush things.

Checklist

- Have your builder verify the platform compaction using a proctor test. Best is over ninety-three percent proctor for a simple platform sitting on bedrock, ninety-five percent or higher for all others.

- Verify that all retaining walls necessary to prevent erosion are in place.

- Walk your build while it's still chalk. Any last minute expansions or changes are best handled at this point.

- Pay attention to the workmanship of the walls. Verify that mortar joints meet code. Confirm good block quality.

- Keep an eye on the schedule versus money paid out. You should be done with *obra negra* by the time you're forty-five percent paid in, roughly. On single story, maybe a bit less.

- Try to get down to the site at least a couple times during *obra negra*. Once, when the platform is chalked, and again, when the walls are going up and before the roof is poured. Plan to get down more often during finishes, maybe once a month, or every six weeks. The more comfortable and familiar you are with the process and the progress, the happier you'll be at the end of the job.

- Look at homes you like, and select an exterior mortar treatment that will wear well and that's consistent with the look you like.

Chapter 6 – Finishes

Overview

It's been said that finishes make or break a house. You can do everything right in *obra negra*, but if the last ten percent of the house is less than well done, the whole thing will look shoddy. Conversely, you can build a lousy *obra negra*, and if you throw money and time at the finishes, that "lipstick on a pig" will translate into a home that shows beautifully.

This chapter will address the finish process, and walk you through the various stages, and attempt to provide insight so that you understand what's being done. It will offer opinion on the right way to do things, will caution against the wrong way, will counsel how to avoid pitfalls, and guide you to what's hopefully a brilliant conclusion to your homebuilding experience.

As we move through the finish stages, I'll throw out some suggestions to improve your final product, and give you some nuts and bolts ways to watch your back to ensure you don't get taken to the cleaners.

One thing to bear in mind as you read this chapter is my statement that the last ten percent of a house's completion can take thirty percent or more of the total build time. When you get into the details of the last ten percent, everything slows to a crawl, as a fine hand is required to get superior results, and oftentimes things need to be done several times to meet quality objectives. Homes in Baja are hand-made, and like all hand-made goods, will be unique, and will be only as good as the hands that are making them.

In the United States, so much is precision cut and pre-fabbed that we take for granted most elements that have to be hand-built when constructed here. Once you've been through the homebuilding process in Baja, you gain tremendous respect for the skills of the craftsmen who ply their trade in the region. You also develop a sense of the unique character each hand-made home will have. There are no two homes identically built here, no two with the exact same craftsmanship or finishes. That's part of the charm.

If your expectation is for a "perfect" home you're going to be disappointed. There's no such thing. All homes, especially hand-made homes, are going to have unique wrinkles and lines, little idiosyncrasies that distinguish each one. The goal is to get as good an example as you can of the quality you paid for, and this chapter will strive to help you do just that.

Plaster – The Start of The Finish

Once *obra negra* is complete, the plaster crew moves in, and starts applying "*yeso*" to all the interior walls. They'll move room to room, standing on ad hoc wooden scaffolding as they use measuring bars to apply the coating of plaster that will be the ultimate "skin" of the interior, just under the paint.

Different builders will use different levels of finish on *yeso* work. I like to apply a full inch of plaster to all interior walls – I've found that it delivers a sonically more appealing result, and the home just feels more solid with all that plaster over the block or foam. There's no ultimate authority on what the best *yeso* thickness is, however I can offer one observation: The thinner the *yeso* coat, the less it costs the builder, as *yeso* is relatively expensive as materials go. Hopefully you specified a thickness on your finish list and *memorio,* and hopefully your list from the builder specifies the tolerance for *yeso* thickness. It should.

This is another one of those things that are fairly easy to verify, with a tape measure. I wouldn't be too concerned if it's 7/8 of an inch in places if the spec calls for an inch, but I would start getting worried if I found most areas with a half inch or less. That would signal time to chitty-chat with the builder.

One finish item you'll be asked about is what the corners should look like. Straight/sharp, a tiny bit of rounding, considerable rounding, etc. Different styles of architecture call for different treatments, so again, there's no right or wrong answer here. I will caution you that if you select straight/sharp, that you don't want to see uneven lines. This is one of those places where you really need to see a straight line, hand-made or not. Otherwise your home is going to look poorly finished. I've walked through homes with supposedly sharp corners, where literally every edge had chips taken out, or it looked like the corners were never finished properly. That always leaves an impression on me, and it's not a positive one.

Some styles don't use *yeso* at all. Some of the contemporary Mexican approaches continue a rougher exterior stucco-like finish into the interior, and it can be very effective. It's more expensive to do than *yeso*, generally, but I do like the look. It's also not to be confused with low-end work, where they just throw some mortar on the inside and paint over it. That's more barrio-level building, and shouldn't appear anywhere where quality is part of the discussion.

You can also select more rustic plaster finishes, where you can see the trowel marks and such. I like these a lot for hacienda-style finishes, as they lend "authentic Mexican" character, and a certain mainland country feel. But they tend to be more expensive to do, so consider carefully that choice before you pull the trigger. I think it's worth it for certain looks, but only you can be the judge of the tradeoffs between cost and appeal.

Same goes for Venetian plaster. It costs more, because it's a two-step process requiring different materials. Again, it can look awesome in certain homes, however you need to get clear on the cost before you give the go-ahead.

There are infinite variations of the plaster topic. Polished finishes, rustic treatments, you name it, they can do it. I think that having some non-traditional surfaces can be a real adder to the unique character of a home, and advise clients that this is one of those areas where a few extra bucks can transform the feel.

Yeso work will take anywhere from three weeks to a month or more. It's not really possible to accelerate the process by adding guys, as they start to get in each others' way if you have too many, and it interferes with the other trades working around them. I like to use one crew of experts to do the entire house, so the same set of hands does every surface. That allows me to ensure uniform quality. But every builder is different.

Flooring

One of the most obvious and critical areas in a house is the floor. Everyone has seen plenty of floors, and it doesn't take an expert to tell whether the workmanship is good or not. Flooring is a key finish that will determine how the home ultimately shows.

The main thing to look for in workmanship is a minimum of lippage – differences in the level of the tile as it's laid down. It's far better to get it right the first time than to have to come back and grind down flooring. Having said that, there's no such thing as a perfect flooring installation, and some post-installation leveling is virtually guaranteed to have to be done. The goal is to minimize that.

Quality of the flooring is a different story. While this book isn't long enough to cover all the factors that impact flooring quality, I can offer some quick and dirty tips that will point you in the right direction.

If you're using marble, just recognize up front that this is a naturally occurring stone, and that there's tremendous variation in most marbles. While it's possible to hand select smaller spaces and get them uniform, you could spend a month on an entire house and still find fault with your choices when you return to reconsider your handiwork. Just understand that you're working with a natural substance that isn't going to be uniform, and you'll stay sane a lot longer. Part of the beauty of natural stone is the variation, so celebrate it instead of condemning it.

If you're using travertine, there are some fairly straightforward guidelines to quality differentiation. First is fill. The amount of fill is generally a decent indicator of the quality. The more fill, the lower the quality. You need to get clear with your builder what his guidelines are for flooring before you start installing or you're setting yourself up for a big letdown. I have a system I use, which is basically establishing a maximum size for any fill I will allow in one of my builds. Any bigger, reject. It's simple to use and easily explainable. The second guideline is color. The lighter the color, the better the quality, although there are exceptions to this rule. Many prefer the more caramel-colored travertines, which can be visually very appealing, especially in more classic or rustic homes. I don't tend to pay a whole lot of attention color-grading travertine based upon what some vendor has established. There are numerous grades of travertine, the top being "super select", which is all I use, thus I usually don't have a lot of problems with color or fill. Still, you have to be vigilant, as vendors will try to slip some lower grade into the shipment. Human nature. My advice, again, is to have clear guidelines with the builder so everyone's expectations are on the same wavelength.

I also will counsel against using tumbled travertine, as while it can look gorgeous, it's a nightmare to clean in the real world. Not to say I wouldn't use it if a client was adamant, however it's a real pain to deal with after the house is turned over, and I try to make that clear up front.

I don't really like to use ceramic tile, even though there are many which are pretty good imitations of real stone. My experience is that ceramic equates to cheapness in many peoples' minds, and I don't really want to spend my time installing flooring that most consider inferior. I've heard all the arguments for using ceramic, however they're all cost arguments – there isn't anyone arguing that mass produced synthetic stone is going to be perceived as higher quality than the genuine article. My sense is to avoid ceramics if you're reading this book, and are considering anything quality oriented. Save it for the tract homes in the United States.

Wood flooring is largely impractical here, due to termites, warping, and cost. The heat plays hell with wood floors, they damage easily, bugs like to eat them, and they cost a fortune compared to stone. Again, you can do whatever you like, but my counsel is avoid the chronic headaches you'll encounter resulting from that choice.

When you think through your flooring, you should also decide what type of *zoclo* you want. *Zoclo* is the kick plate of stone running the periphery of the room, usually advancing four to six inches or so up the wall. There are two ways to do it – extruded, or flush with the wall. I like flush, as it's a cleaner look, however there's no right answer here. Just make sure it gets defined before they start installing, as often the builder just makes the decision for you.

We don't need to discuss patterns here, as you already should have covered that with your designer in the plan stage. If you didn't, my advice is to get a flooring design done with a pro, and make it part of the onsite plans the maestro will follow and supervise. I hate oral traditions, as they lend themselves to interpretation, and thus error. Put it in writing, and then there's no interpretation necessary.

A parting comment. Larger flooring has more impact, but costs more – often way more. Still, flooring sets the tone of the house, so it may be worth balancing cost with first impressions. Working with larger tiles has its own drawbacks, as they tend to be more expensive to install along with the higher raw material cost, and you see more breakage. You also have to be sensitive to the thicker tile, and make allowances for it when you're contemplating the installation. But if you can afford it, bigger really is better when it comes to flooring.

Steps

One of my pet peeves is stairways or steps where the height varies from step to step. It's so avoidable, and yet probably eighty-five percent of the homes in Baja have uneven stairs. The reason this is bad is that the body automatically adjusts to stairs, and it expects the next step to be the same as the last, especially going down stairs. If the distance is different by more than a nominal amount, say, less than a quarter inch or so, there's a good chance that someone is going to fall down those stairs. Just a matter of time.

In *obra negra*, steps can be off by a fair amount, however at finish time, they should be carefully measured, and brought to a uniform height. That isn't so tough to do, actually, and involves using a measuring tape.

The problem is that many *Maestros* don't bother with the measuring tape part, resulting in the uneven stair effect.

You can and should check stairs at this stage, using your own measuring tape. If you suspect that they aren't going to be even once completed, bring the builder into it, as it's very fast and easy to get it right from the inception, and difficult to fix it after the fact.

Note that the top step, or any landings, will be different in *obra negra* due to allowances for the mortar and the flooring. That's why I bring it up here, and not in *obra negra* – making the *Maestro's* life miserable over slight discrepancies at that stage in unproductive, however at this stage, as you're into the finishes, it's appropriate to voice concern. Again, you aren't questioning anyone's competence, you're simply verifying tolerances. If they're off, call it here, as it will be too late down the road a bit.

Roof

At some point, usually while the *yeso* guys are doing the plastering, the crew will be working on the exterior while all the work's going on in the interior. One of the things they'll be doing is roofing.

The first step is to waterproof the roof area with special waterproofing paint, a sealer, really, to keep the water out. Concrete is bad as far as water goes, in that water will find even the smallest cracks or fissures, and work its way to the interior from there. It's critically important that the waterproofing is done methodically, and comprehensively. If it didn't only rain here less than a dozen days per year, it would be far easier to tell how many of the homes going up are actually storm-worthy, however we are blessed with extraordinary weather, so we only get to test things once a year. Add to the mix that heat and sun destroy everything with time, and you can see how roofs and waterproofing are weak links in the chain. Another tip is to use the most expensive waterproofing you can get your hands on – there honestly is a big difference between the budget ones and the high-end ones, at least in my experience.

The next step is to apply the *teja* tile to the roof (assuming it's a sloped roof with tile, and not a flat roof. Flat roofs receive the water proofing, and then are either painted, or sealed with a topcoat of nonskid material so guests can walk around on them). This is pretty straightforward as well. Row after row of tiles are set in place with mortar, to hold them down when the big winds hit. On the mainland, in many places they don't bother to mortar them down, as the areas don't get hit with hurricanes, however here, it's a must.

You should take a look at your roof once it's done and confirm that there are no cracked or broken tiles, as it's not uncommon for workers to damage some, but neglect to say anything or replace them. Only takes a minute to look at them, and it will save a lot of pain and suffering once the hurricanes hit and water deluges the roof.

Another pet peeve of mine is unsightly PVC vent pipes which many builders leave sticking out of their roofs. A few builders even make the eyesores worse by creating jointed and angled pipes, of course leaving them white, so they completely destroy the look of the roof. My solution is to paint the pipes as close to the roof color as possible, and structure them as unobtrusively as possible, so that it doesn't look like barrio row housing technique on a million dollar roof treatment. You might want to have a discussion about this when the roof is laid so that you get a reasonable aesthetic effect, rather than a cheap-white-pipe-fest on your dream home.

AC

Once the plaster work is done, the air conditioning equipment will go in. If you have gone with Fan & Coil, this is where the large units that go in at the ceiling level are delivered and mounted.

When installed, ductwork will be run from the units to the various areas each unit cools. You want to make sure that there's both a duct for the exhaust, which is the cool air, as well as for the intake. Some builders just leave the intake without a duct, which is a recipe for disaster, as the air the unit sucks in will then come from the intake grid, through the dust and residue that sits in the airspace between the sheetrock ceiling and the concrete ceiling, and ultimately clog the unit up with gunk. With a grid and duct, the air comes through the grid and down the duct, protected from the dust and grit, ensuring a longer life for your unit. This is one of those easy things to ask your builder about, and to insist on.

Once the ducts are run, a sheetrock or plastered ceiling will be installed, to hide all the ducts and the actual unit. Most builders put the units in bathrooms or in closet areas, as the lower ceilings are unobtrusive in those spaces. The final touch will be to plaster over the sheetrock, creating the appearance of a natural ceiling consistent with the rest of the home. They'll leave a hatch in each area, to get to the AC units.

Make sure you discuss with your builder where you want the thermostat in each room, as each "zone" will require its own on/off and temp control unit on the wall. Best to have it near the bed in the bedrooms so you don't have to get up in the middle of the night to change the temp.

If you're using mini-splits, the builder will run tubing for the condensation, as well as conduit, up each wall to the location the plastic appliance will hang. There's no drop ceiling and no ducts, just the unit on the wall, which also contains the thermostat.

As part of the testing of the home, make sure the builder tests the AC before the home is completed and turned over. That way, if something is wrong, you have time to correct it before you take possession.

Exterior Rock

If your design has exterior rockwork articulated on it, you'll get to see it go on around this stage. What you should know is that there are different grades of stonework, each carrying a different cost.

The most typical is where the stone has mortar in the joints. That's the most economical, and the most widely used, as it looks good and can be completed quickly. The next most expensive is where the mortar joints are filled with smaller rocks, creating a sort of artful look to the stone – but that takes considerably longer to do, due to all the detail. The most expensive sort of stonework is one where no mortar is visible, and the stones seem to fit seamlessly next to each other. That can take three times longer to do, and it not unexpectedly carries a considerably higher cost than either of the other alternatives. Examples of this expensive sort of stonework can be seen on the beach in Puerto Los Cabos, as well as in Palmilla.

Hopefully you've discussed these differences with your builder in advance of the stonework being done. Unless it has been specifically called out, you can expect the most widely used type to be the norm on your house. It's not really fair to demand a level of fit on the stonework beyond the norm, unless that has been paid for or articulated in the bid as such.

Lighting and Electrical

There isn't much you need to do as the electrical goes in, other than to specify the color of the switch plates and the types of lamps to be used in each area. Generally, the builder will have standard cans he uses, that were specified in the bid.

If you want special lights above mirrors or over vanities, you should discuss with the builder your selection well in advance, as well as confirm placement before too much gets installed. If you have the lights installed per the electrical plan, and then decide to change anything spatially, that will be a change order, so try to think through the exact placements before the cabinets and granite go in.

Same goes for lighting in cabinet areas. If you decide to do this, decide early, and ensure conduit makes it to the areas you want lighting. This is especially important for items like under-cabinet lighting.

The builder will test all outlets and switches as he goes along, and also as part of his final pass through before he hands over the keys. So what you're mainly looking for here is to ensure that whatever is on the plan makes it into the house. It isn't your obligation to do so, but spot checking a few critical areas is never a bad idea, if just to confirm for yourself that everything is as it should be.

One item of note is that you'll need to run all your computers, cable boxes, and appliances, via surge protectors, or you risk frying them. Anything with a microprocessor in it should be on a surge protector. The area is rife with brownouts and power spikes, which no builder can protect against. You need to make sure all your equipment is protected from this phenomena, or the builder is just going to shrug his shoulders when your stuff starts frying – there's nothing he can do.

And finally, you'll want to have outlets with breakers on them in all bathrooms. Wherever there's electricity and water, there should be breaker outlets so you don't wind up frying yourself.

Paint

Once the roof is on, and the trim around the roof is done, it will be time to paint the exterior, followed by the interior.

First, a primer coat will go onto the entire house.

At this stage, you absolutely should plan to be in town, as you'll need to actually see the paint color you have selected as a sample on the house. The reason to be here in person is that paint can look different on larger areas, and especially on concrete walls. Make absolutely sure that the paint is applied over a primer coat, as the primer will change the color of the paint – you want to see a literal example of the way the paint will look on your house, not a sample on concrete that will look completely different once primer is applied.

Also, paint type is a big deal, as different brands and quality levels within a brand will define what the paint winds up wearing like. I prefer Sherwin Williams, however that's just because I've had consistent experiences with the brand. Other builders swear by other brands. It's all a matter of preference, and of course, cost.

As far as exterior painting goes, again, there's not a lot of ways you can screw it up, other than to put the windows in before you paint, and then slop paint all over them. I've seen a number of homes where that's the finished product, and it's completely avoidable by putting the windows in after the paint is done, or by carefully taping off the frames so you don't get a bunch of overspray or seepage. It's way faster and easier to just do it correctly the first time, and to take reasonable precautions, rather than having to do things over repeatedly, or spend weeks cleaning up avoidable messes.

One item to watch for is that the paint is applied evenly, and they don't miss any spots. Sounds obvious, but you'd be surprised.

Same basic message applies to interior paint – you want to see a neat, orderly paint job, where proper prep work is done, and where the coats go on evenly, with no slop. The tendency is to want to cut corners, and not tape properly, or take appropriate precautions with covering floors and such. That results in a sloppy job, with paint on undesirable surfaces, and with unpleasant edging. It only takes a bit more time to do it correctly the first time.

As an aside, I like to do hacienda style and mission style homes with sponge painted exteriors, whenever possible. It costs more, but it gives a rustic, seasoned look to the home that has enormous appeal if done tastefully. I also like to do rag painting or sponge painting on interiors to add warmth and dimension. I don't like seeing sponge painting used to cover up exterior defects in the mortar, however, which is all too common around here, especially on panel homes, as the trained eye will still spot the flaws. If you're not sure about it, my advice is to first paint the home a flat color, and then make the call on sponge painting.

Windows and Iron

I wait until the house is painted to put windows in. That's to cut down on the chances of slopping paint all over the frames, and also as a function of how I like to stage the trades.

Let me say right up front that there are two trades that will generally be a problem in Baja. The first is windows, the second is carpentry. I have no idea why these two trades are such problems, but they are, and you're hereby forewarned.

What kinds of problems can occur? Well, we can start with the basics – the seals around the glass in the windows. I've seen terrible seal work on the majority of homes in Cabo, mainly caused by using the wrong seals for the job, or using one type for all applications. Both are easily corrected by getting the right material, and you'd think that would occur to professionals who earn their living by making and installing windows, however you'd be amazed once you've walked through enough new builds to know the lay of the land.

I can't tell you how often I've had to go back, with a specialist, to redo seals once the window company has finished the installation. It's just one of those things that nobody seems to be able to avoid, unless they import windows from the States, or Europe – and then they have to contend with the inevitable imperceptible but important variations in size that are a function of building out of concrete, or by hand. Most windows are hand-made onsite, using material shipped in from the mainland, and as with all hand-made items, there will be variations in outcome. Additionally, when the windows are installed, it's easy to be lackadaisical about being precise with the silicone sealant that goes around the frames. That will translate into major water damage when the first big storm hits. Best to pay attention to that work now, rather than discovering it via ruined plaster and cracked paint after a hurricane.

The second thing that surfaces is using improper parts for a given job. "Jury rigging" is a time honored pastime in Baja, and the locals are very resourceful at innovating ways to solve problems without the correct part, however it's a lousy way to install things like pocket doors or windows. This can result in rattling pocket doors, in rattling windows, in windows that howl at night in the wind – you name it.

As an example of these types of issues coming into play on a project, I did a walkthrough of a competitor's place in one of the big marquis communities a few months back, and was struck by the client's persistent complaints about problems with bugs and critters constantly in their home, no matter what was sprayed or done to prevent them from entering. Having some experience with these sorts of things, I went over to the pocket doors, and looked down each side, where the doors slid into the wall cavity. When closed, I reached my hand around the frame, and waggled my fingers – there was an easy four inches of space on either side, with nothing to keep the AC in, or the critters out. What had happened was that the builder and the windows guys had either forgotten, or didn't realize that they needed, a metal flap that pops out to seal off the airspace to prevent bugs from getting in. The flap was missing, hence the problem. Easy to fix with the right part, but it had been a problem for the client for half a year, with no solution in sight. Mind boggling, but there it is. Most problems here are like that – simple to solve, but many go unsolved for long periods.

All of these issues come down to supervision at the time the windows and doors are being installed. Often, the owner of the window company is off hustling new business, so the workers are left unsupervised to put the stuff in the best they can. They, lacking any incentive to really care how good or bad a job they do, will take the path of least resistance, and do whatever is easiest. It's a good idea to speak with your builder and voice the concern about the quality you expect on the windows and doors – if additional attention is brought to bear on that discipline at the installation phase, it will make everyone's life easier than if the windows need to be worked on at the end of the job. Again, expecting the sort of precision and quality you would get in the United States in a factory-built window is counter-productive unless you pay the extra to import United States factory-built windows, which can almost double your window cost here. So it's better to have a realistic idea of what can be done here, and then strive to get it done as best as can be given the limitations inherent in hand making the frames at the site.

But it's not unreasonable to want to have windows that are water-tight, and that don't rattle, and that don't let in bugs. It's also not unreasonable to want windows that look good, and that are competently installed. Focus on that, and have it as your objective, and you should be fine.

Terraces and Decks

Once all the interior flooring is done, it's usually time to turn to laying the exterior terraces and deck surfaces. These go down pretty quickly, unless there are ornate patterns or trims involved. The main thing to confirm is that there are appropriate slopes to the surfaces so water will run off and drain when it rains. This can be easily accomplished using a level.

As mentioned earlier, I tend to use cantera for my deck surfaces, as it stays cool in the sun, is a natural stone, and is wheelchair friendly. I'll put in 16 X 16 inch (40 X 40 cm) squares, which wear well, and are larger and better quality than the commercial grade stuff that comes in 12 X 12 inch (30 X 30 cm) squares.

Cantera is a naturally occurring sedimentary stone that comes in a variety of shades, anywhere from greenish white, to chocolate brown. It's characterized by mineral deposits and sediment, and it's typically a very soft stone. So soft that you can scratch it with virtually anything harder than a fingernail. Not a problem, however, as it tends to last adequately on outdoor surfaces, and is non-skid.

You'll want to seal it once the cantera is laid, and probably want to come back once a year and re-seal it, as the seal wears off over time. It is very porous, so sealing is a must.

I avoid outdoor surfaces like rock, as rock gets white hot in the summer, and is tough on bare feet year-round, however there are some builders who use rock and seem to like it. Personal preference, I suppose, but if you've ever stubbed your toe on rock, or watched someone try to use a walker or wheelchair on it, you'll immediately understand why I consider it to be a drawback, and an impractical surface.

At this point, the ironwork will also get installed – or at least it will once the terraces are done. Ironwork in Baja is rarely if ever powder coated. Rather, it's primer coated, and then painted. The issue is that there are only a couple of places to get things powder coated, and cost makes it prohibitive. If the primer is done correctly, and then the paint is applied correctly, it should last for years before requiring any sort of maintenance.

Pools and Jacuzzis

If you're going to do a swimming pool, your biggest choice will be the type of surfacing to use. It's really a choice of tile, or pebbletech. The second big choice will be fresh or salt water.

Before the pool gets surfaced, you'll want to fill it with water and wait a week to see if there are any leaks. Leaks abound in Cabo, due to the seismic activity, as well as the effect of the sun on concrete, however the largest source of leakage is usually the light fixtures in the pool, and the pipes. The builder will want to pressure test all the pipes and verify that there are no leaks, and then fill the pool with water and see what happens. If all is well after a week, they'll drain it, and start on the surfacing.

Tile can be a colorful and appealing choice. The downside with it is that over time, you can expect to lose some tiles. It's also slippery, so any sort of sloped area is a danger zone with tile. I like to use it for infinity edges on pools, and as a border touch on pebbletech pools.

Pebbletech is a coarse sand-grain finish that's available in a number of colors. It's more expensive to apply than tile, however it only takes a day or so to shoot a pool, whereas tile can take three weeks or more to apply. The positives are that it's non-slip and durable, and when labor is taken into account, is about the same net cost as tile. The negative is that it usually looks a bit blotchy regardless of which company applies it.

Most of my pools are done in pebbletech as clients prefer that finish, as do I. I can live with the blotchiness inherent to the material as a reasonable tradeoff for all the positives.

On your Jacuzzi, if you have one, you'll face all the same issues. Your builder will need to test the pumps and jets to confirm they all work, and that there are no leaks. Again, this is pretty straightforward stuff, so not a lot of heavy lifting required from you at this stage.

Carpentry

Wood. Doors and cabinets, the shining star of the home's interior. Or at least that's the way it should be.

I wait until everything else in the house is done before I start on carpentry installation. The only items left when I bring the wood in are the granite counters, for which I need the carpentry boxes in place, and exterior items, and interior touch ups. This is because it's so easy to damage wood – every time a worker hits it with a tool, or dings it with a ladder, or drops something on it, it gets damaged, resulting in additional costs.

Carpentry is the most visible element in the home, besides the floor. Ensuring a quality job is imperative. The rub is that carpentry is also the toughest trade to deal with in Baja, and the least given to any efforts at quality control, or scheduling. Carpenters are the bane of many builders' existences, and I don't see that changing any time soon.

That said, you'll want to look at some obvious items and confirm decent fit and finish. First, look at the hinges once the doors are hung – are the hinges morticed (that's where they recess the hinges flush with the wood doorframe, as opposed to just screwing down the hinge to the surface of the wood)? If not, they should be.

Are the joints on the cabinets cleanly executed? Do the cabinets follow the carpentry plan? This can seem like an obvious one, however you'd be shocked how many cabinets show up and are nothing like what was ordered. I'm talking wrong dimensions, drawers where doors were supposed to be, etc.

Assuming that everything is the right size and configuration, look at the finishes. Are they the correct color? How did you establish the correct color in the first place? I try to get clients to sign off on a sample of the type of wood they'll use, with the exact color and product to be used, so there's a control piece to compare the deliverables to. Are the surfaces cleanly executed, or do they look badly made? Are the cabinet faces and drawer faces what was ordered? Are they evenly spaced? Again, the carpentry plan should have the design and pattern articulated so there's no ambiguity, or alternatively, there should be a drawing signed off articulating the pattern and look you want. What about the drawer pulls? Are those the correct ones?

Do all the drawers open and close correctly? How about the doors? Are they straight? Do they work correctly? How about the interiors of the cabinets? Are they finished well? Are the correct number of shelves in place, in the right spots? If you have an island, are the undersides of the supports for the granite tops stained, or left as raw plywood? They should be stained.

When you go over your carpentry, you need to look not only for blemishes, but to confirm correct configuration and fit. Confirm that the box fronts are the same color as the doors and drawers. Confirm that closets are the correct configurations, and that all doors and drawers function as intended.

Last but not least, open all room doors, and see if they'll hit walls or cabinets. If so, have your builder put in door stops so that nothing is damaged. And also confirm that the appropriate doors have keyed locks or privacy locks. You'll want them on all bathrooms, and keyed locks on the garage door, the front door, and any exterior doors as well as any doors to areas you hope to keep private when the home is full of guests, or rented out.

Granite

At the point the carpentry boxes are in, the granite countertops can be installed. They're usually cut offsite, and then installed over a period of a week or two once the boxes are in place.

There isn't much for you as a client to do at this stage other than to confirm that the correct granite was delivered, and that there are no obvious flaws. You might want to confirm that the sinks are correctly spaced, and that the faucets get placed where you want them, but other than that, this phase is largely hands off.

One caveat: The darker the granite, the more obvious the seams will be. No way around it, unfortunately. I try to steer clients in the direction of lighter colors, as no granite vendor will guarantee that the seams meet client approval on the darker colors.

Fixtures and Appliances & Hot Water

Once the granite is on, you're nearing the finish line. The next step will be finish plumbing, wherein the faucets are mounted, the sinks are connected, and your appliances are put into place.

The main thing to watch for at this stage is that nobody lost any of the faucets or shower faucets or tub faucets. Assuming that they're all there, you'll also want to confirm that the toilets are installed and functioning. Ditto for the tubs if they're Jacuzzi tubs.

This may sound obvious, but one of the greatest sources of initial client complaints is a lack of familiarity with how to operate new shower faucets to get hot water. Probably one of the next most common is being unfamiliar with how pilot lights work, as well as propane tanks.

Familiarize yourself with the location of your propane tank, and if you're unsure, ask about your pilot lights on your hot water heaters. Also, confirm which heater serves which part of the house if you have more than one. That way if there are any issues once you've taken possession, you can quickly determine if there's some sort of operator error, or if there's a genuine equipment issue.

Once the appliances are installed and hooked up to utilities, you or the builder should verify that everything is working as expected. Infant mortality is not unheard of on items shipped down the Baja highway, so don't assume that anything is intact. Test the dishwasher, the microwave, the fridge, the oven. I would say that I see some sort of infant mortality issue at least twenty-five percent of the time, so this isn't a hollow warning. Learn where the gas shutoff valve is for the oven and cook top, as well as which breakers operate the kitchen appliances. You'll be glad you did should the unexpected occur.

Driveways, Garage Doors, Exterior Flourishes

You're almost at the end of the road now – all that remains is to complete the driveway, install the garage door, go through the house with a pickup crew to cover details, and complete the exterior flourishes and specialty items.

When the garage door is installed, confirm that it opens correctly, and that the motor and track are installed securely. Same for the side tracks – they should be sturdily attached. Also confirm that the on/off wall switch is mounted close to the entry door from the home.

Most of the time, garage doors are metal, rather than wood. Wood garage doors look good, but they tend to be prone to the same swelling and shrinking issues that all other exterior wood is, thus are maintenance headaches. I tend to discourage using any exterior wood in operational areas like a garage door, as harsh experience has taught me that it invites ongoing problems.

There isn't too much to address on doing a driveway – it's either installed well and to plan, or it isn't. Same for all the exterior flourishes and finishing touches on the interior. You're now no more than a week or so from having the home done, so if you're reading this and are at this stage with your project, you're in the last one percent of the house.

While the exterior items are being completed, a pick-up crew will go room by room, and address any paint, plaster, grout, or flooring issues. The goal is to have the place livable and complete once the keys are handed over. The pick-up crew is the last step in finishing up the home.

Hurricane Protection

I get asked all the time what I think of various hurricane protection solutions, and whether it's worth buying any of them. My philosophy is that it's kind of like a seatbelt or car insurance – you hope you never need them, but it sure is nice that you have them should something terrible happen.

Reality is that most homes go through the hurricane season here with no damage other than leaks that sprout up over the long sunny year of having the roof and the window seals baking in hundred degree heat. A friend of mine who's been here for over two decades tells me that he's only seen one window blow in during that time. More often, what happens is flying debris hits windows and breaks them, or loose windows rattle and break in the high winds.

Having said that, it's not such a bad idea to batten down the hatches and put something between you and the storm. Steel is good. I don't have a ton of data to evaluate the latest rage, which is the Kevlar product that acts as a transparent barrier between the storm and your glass, but I understand the theory, and it seems reasonable. My only problem is that to come into play, your window has to blow in first, and then the protection starts. With steel, the window never breaks. That sounds better to me…

My sense is that if you have the money to get hurricane protection on at least the windows and pocket doors that face the ocean, why not? It's worth it just for the peace of mind.

Checklist

- *Yeso*. Inspect plaster, confirm thickness and corners.

- Flooring. Confirm flooring quality and workmanship.

- Stairs and Steps.

- Roof. Ensure waterproofing done prior to tile application, confirm tiles mortared in place.

- Electric. Verify everything according to plan.

- Paint. Color confirmation only after primer coat under sample.

- Windows. Confirm seals, silicone, workmanship.

- Terraces. Inspect workmanship, verify slopes.

- Pool and Jacuzzi. Make sure no leaks, all systems work.

- Carpentry. Inspect, verify correctly configured, good fit and finish.

- Fixtures. Confirm all there, functional.

- Driveway & Garage Door. Confirm competently installed.

- Hurricane Protection.

Chapter 7 – End Game

Overview

At this point, you've spent the last year or so building your home, and likely at least another half a year or more in the planning phase. It's all paid off now, and manifest in concrete and steel is the home you've put so much energy and money into.

Take a deep breath, and congratulate yourself. You've taken a journey few take, and if you've followed the counsel in this guide, have avoided most if not all of the nightmares that can be part and parcel of the process.

Now it's no longer a project, but rather a dream become reality.

This final chapter is intended to give you a framework for orienting yourself with your home, structuring the inevitable warranty repair visits, dealing with the paperwork you'll have to retain or file, and assimilating some tips on the associated tasks you'll need to tackle as you move in and make the home yours.

Before we get into the detail, let me share with you the observation that there's no such thing as a perfect home. No matter how much time you spend designing it, and no matter how meticulous the builder, there will be things you'll wish you'd done differently, or that the builder had done better. That's normal. The key to having a good experience is in understanding the limitations of the area, and being satisfied that your home is as good as it could be for the money. Again, you can compare your place to homes that cost $500 a foot to build, but what's the point? If you didn't pay that much, it's like comparing your car to a $500,000 Porsche. The comparison isn't germane, or appropriate.

I will say that I've walked through a few of the $500 per foot places, and even on those I can find plenty of things I would have done differently, or thought were sloppy or unfinished or rough. There isn't a home in Baja I couldn't do that with, as again, hand-made homes are idiosyncratic, and will always have their own flaws and ticks. My point is that the whole exercise is to get the best home you can for the money you paid – a competently built home that meets the quality expectations you set when evaluating what your budget would get you. Don't fall into the trap of nitpicking every square inch, or you'll drive yourself crazy, and your builder will stop taking your calls. There's reasonable, and there's obsessive compulsive. If slight imperfections drive you 'round the bend, you shouldn't be building anything in Baja, or probably anywhere else, for that matter, as the nature of the beast building custom homes is that there will be traits that lend the home "personality."

As an example, one potential client expressed disappointment with a $12 million home in Querencia, and felt that he could get better quality for the lower end of the high quality range – the very low end of that range, as in about a third of what the Querencia place cost to build. That always gives me pause, as I question what the secret sauce is that he thinks he'll introduce to get the deal that nobody else here has been able to get. To me, that's a really unhappy client ready to happen – the expectations aren't realistic, so it's a disaster in the making. I can see lawsuits on that horizon, as unrealistic expectations encounter the harsh reality of the Baja dirt, and the quality's found to be lacking. That isn't to say that you can't get high quality here, but the idea is to educate yourself and get adequate context for your expectations so that you aren't setting yourself up for a big come down. If you heeded my advice, and did your homework, this isn't you. Hopefully you did. If so, you'll be far better off with your Mexican home experience.

That doesn't mean you should accept substandard or shoddily built construction, but it also doesn't mean that you should make it your life's work to find every inch of possible imperfection. The goal of this book was to get you a nice home built to competent standards and high quality, with a minimum of fuss or headache. If you've been diligent in the application of each chapter's advice, you got what you wanted, and now all that's left is to do your walkthrough and pick up the keys.

The Walkthrough

When you walk through the home with the builder, you should bear in mind that you won't come close to catching all the niggling items you'll want taken care of as part of the warranty. That's not the goal of the walkthrough.

What you should be trying to achieve is to confirm that all the systems are operational, that everything looks good on first blush, and that the home is livable and finished. To that end, what follows is a list of items I tend to think are the critical items you should be checking.

1. Confirm that chemicals are in treatment plant.

2. Confirm gas is in propane tank.

3. Verify all doors latch, and that locks are keyed correctly.

4. Verify that all lights work.

5. Verify that all AC units function.

6. Confirm hot water at all taps.

7. Confirm garage door opens, and that remotes are in hand.

8. Confirm that all fans work.

9. Verify that all appliances operational.

10. Confirm that all windows are complete and latch properly.

11. Same for all pocket and sliding doors.

12. Confirm mosquito netting on all windows and doors.

13. Confirm exterior lights working.

14. Flush all toilets and confirm they work.

15. Verify that flooring and paint complete and to reasonable quality.

16. Verify that finish cabinetry acceptable.

17. Verify that breaker panel is complete, and labeled.

18. Familiarize yourself with pool equipment operation.

19. Familiarize yourself with water pump system and confirm adequate pressure at the taps.

20. Verify that exterior look finished and all gross items are complete.

21. Put surge protectors on all appliances and electric devices containing a microprocessor.

As you can see, this is broad strokes, nuts and bolts stuff. You want to ensure that the home is ready for occupation, and that all systems work correctly. You also want to make completely sure that you understand how things work, because once you take the keys, it's your house, and not the builder's project. That can seem a little scary, but if you've done even half the things outlined in this book's pages, you'll be OK.

Part of the handoff is also to get the paperwork you'll need to keep on hand. The most important document will be the proof of payment of INSS, which is Mexican Social Security. You should keep that socked away in a safe place, as it's not unknown for the SS guys to appear four years after the build is done, and fine you big time should you not have the proof that the SS was paid. I would hold onto it for five years. Longer, if you like.

Another item you'll want to get is the book the DRO signs off on, which lists all the changes and work that was done when the house was built. That's another mandatory item.

You'll also need the *Termination of Obra* letter from *Obras Publicas*, however that can take weeks to months for *Obras Publicas* to issue, so it won't be part of the handoff after the walkthrough.

And you absolutely need to get all the remote controls for every fan and AC unit in the home, along with the aforementioned garage door openers. And all the warranty cards and manuals for all the appliances and AC units and pumps and systems.

Oh, and of course, the keys to the house.

At this juncture, the builder is going to want to get his final payment. That's reasonable, as he's done his job. While some will try to hold off on paying until they've spent some time in the house, that's unreasonable unless the contract specifies it as a condition. That's where the warranty comes in – to handle any defects you discover after you occupy the home. At the point you occupy the home, you own it and the builder's done his job, except for warranty repairs. Mexican law backs the builder up on this, so it would be unwise to push the envelope on the final payment unless you reject the home at the walkthrough and declare it unfinished. Again, if you've been following the counsel in these pages, you shouldn't have any issues that would be deal killers by this point, having caught them all far in advance of the final walkthrough.

Post-Occupancy Punch-list

Once you've occupied the home for a while, you're bound to discover things that need fixing, or that don't measure up to your expectations. Examples might be missing grout, or leaky faucets, or loose windows, or creaky cabinets. My advice is that you have an agreement with your builder to send in a pick-up crew after a month, and then at the end of the first year's occupation. The reason you'll want him out there after a month or so is because you'll have gathered all the first impression issues together and they'll be ready to be taken care of. You'll want to see him again at the end of a year because that's the end of the warranty period, and you'll need all the issues that have come up over the year to be taken care of before you're out of warranty.

What I advise my clients to do for the warranty repairs is to create a checklist, by room, and list the issues accordingly. That way, the crew can go room by room, and have a coherent and clear idea of what they're to do. It will also help the builder, as he can then manage what trades need to be present to address all the concerns. Checklists are your friend. I believe in them, to the point that each chapter ends with…a checklist.

Health Care, Security, Utilities, Property Management

Now that you're in the house, I would strongly advise that you compile a list of critical phone numbers and contacts. You'll need them sooner or later, and best to have them in one place. Get recommendations on dependable healthcare nearby, and have the number of a twenty-four hour clinic handy should bad things happen. Also get the number of a twenty-four hour pharmacy, as well as a service that will deliver medications to your door.

Introduce yourself to the security guards at the gate, assuming you have guards, and get the number to the guard house, as well as the name of the supervisor. You'll be glad you have these handy if you ever suspect someone is breaking in, or whenever you want friends to be allowed in to visit.

Jot down the numbers and addresses of key places, like the power company (CFE), the telephone company (Telmex), the water company, the gas company, the provider of your sewage treatment plant, your landscaper or gardener, a handyman, a plumber, an electrician, a mechanic, the pool guy, a fumigator, and your housekeeper.

I'd also advise those not intending to live full time in their homes, to look hard at professional property management. There are a lot of ways things can go wrong in a home while you're away, and having experienced eyes watching your place is a prudent step. Someone has to pay the bills, and make sure the pool is being cleaned and the plants watered, and fix any broken windows or damaged items on the exterior, and if there's a burst pipe that the water is sopped up and the pipe repaired and not left to fester for months, etc.

I don't offer that service, but I have trustworthy folks who do it, and I seriously advise my clients to build it into their budgets. Dust will build up quickly even when you aren't around, the place will still need to be sprayed for bugs, systems will need to be run, and if you aren't here, someone needs to do it. Either line it up now, or learn the hard way when you've tried to manage things from a thousand miles away.

In Closing

I could keep going for hours, offering tips and advice on the myriad things you'll encounter now that you have a home here, however that's a different book. Hopefully you've found the counsel set forth in this one helpful in its stated purpose, and feel more confident that you understand the process now, and what's required of everyone involved. I can't say often enough that building in Baja can be richly rewarding, both financially as well as from a personal standpoint, however there are very real obstacles that one needs to understand in order to prevail. By now you know most of the major ones, and some of the minor ones. This isn't an exhaustive list by any means, however it beats what has thus far been available – a few columns in the *Gringo Gazette*, and a spotty oral tradition.

The goal of the book is to help you tackle building in Baja. As I said in the first few lines, a sort of "Building in Baja for Dummies" primer for those wishing to build a dream home in what I consider paradise. If you followed the advice in these chapters, you should do well with it, and have a relatively seamless experience. That's the objective.

In the meantime, should you have any questions or observations or suggestions on how this primer can be improved, feel free to contact me by e-mail, at Phil@BuildCabo.com – the book is a changing work in progress, and I suspect there will be more editions with significant improvements and updates.

Thanks for taking the time to take this journey with me. I hope it sets you on the path armed with enough info to be truly dangerous. Drop me a line and let me know if you build a house and find the info helpful – I know this won't be a best seller given the small audience, but I do want to know if I was able to help folks navigate the occasionally treacherous waters of the Baja building scene. If I've been able to do that with any success the time invested served its purpose.

ABOUT THE AUTHOR:

C. Phil Osso is an acclaimed home designer and builder located in Cabo San Lucas, Mexico, who was the featured home construction columnist for the *Gringo Gazette* for 45 issues. His company, BuildCabo Custom Home Design & Construction, builds a select number of luxury homes every year. More information about the author can be found at the company website, BuildCabo.com.